MARKETING

IN THE

PARTICIPATION

AGE

MARKETING
IN THE
PARTICIPATION
AGE

A Guide to Motivating People to Join, Share, Take Part, Connect, and Engage

Daina Middleton

WILEY

John Wiley & Sons, Inc.

Cover image: © Aydin Buyuktas/Alamy

Cover design: Wendy Mount

Published by John Wiley & Sons, Inc., Hoboken, New Jersey.
Published simultaneously in Canada.

For general information on our other products and services or for technical support, please contact our Customer Care Department within the United States at (800) 762-2974, outside the United States at (317) 572-3993 or fax (317) 572-4002.

Wiley publishes in a variety of print and electronic formats and by print-on-demand. Some material included with standard print versions of this book may not be included in e-books or in print-on-demand. If this book refers to media such as a CD or DVD that is not included in the version you purchased, you may download this material at http://book support.wiley.com. For more information about Wiley products, visit www.wiley.com.

ISBN: 978-1-118-40230-6 (cloth)
ISBN: 978-1-118-43195-5 (ebk)
ISBN: 978-1-118-43196-2 (ebk)
ISBN: 978-1-118-43197-9 (ebk)

Printed in the United States of America

10 9 8 7 6 5 4 3 2 1

CONTENTS

FOREWORD

Today's marketers face being overwhelmed with the challenge of how to understand and use the new and dynamic methods and channels of engagement with consumers. With her unique experience and insight, Daina Middleton develops an approach that demonstrates how to connect with individuals and groups through participation. Daina's passion for participant marketing was developed through her leadership roles at some of the world's most respected marketing organizations. The theory and practicality is developed into a robust and highly applicable participation framework.

Marketing in the Participation Age provides an approach for motivating consumers to connect, engage, and socialize, which ultimately results in improved return on investment from marketing investments.

This book is both provocative and informative. It is vital reading for anyone setting out to navigate marketing in a digital age.

—**Steve King**
Global CEO
Zenith Optimedia

ACKNOWLEDGMENTS

My very first recollection of wanting to write a book came when I was just eight years old. At the time, I imagined it would be a historical fiction novel that involved a girl and at least one horse. I still keep a number of stories I began back then in the hopes that I might someday complete them. I never thought I would write a book about marketing until 2007, when I became passionate about discovering new methods for a new age and began using the phrase *participant marketing* to describe a new approach. I first acquired the "participant marketing" URL in 2007, and I am a bit self-conscious to admit that it has taken me five years to complete this project. Beyond the research required to discover the science behind motivating participation, and the historian exercise of learning about our industry, the process was largely transforming conversations from Power Point documents into the written word. Then, there was the journey of reacquainting myself with the writer in me, who is never satisfied with the end product of a subject in which the world is continually changing beneath our feet. I finally became comfortable with the fact that books are thought starters, more than perfect masterpieces, and getting the idea out there is more important than perfectly completing the idea. In the Age of Participation, the idea will continue on not just with my own evolution of the idea, but also with yours, as we all contribute to evolve the idea.

Many people contributed to this original version. This book would not have been possible without a phenomenal group of individuals who provided trust, support, encouragement, faith, and patience along the way. I would like to thank my husband, Rob, for his loving support, encouragement, and patience throughout this project and my children, Mesa, Kenyon, and Brett, for insisting that I could complete the project.

I am forever grateful to Kris Pinto and Joel Lunenfeld for allowing me to experiment with the participant marketing philosophy and methods at Moxie Interactive and to Jon Wegman for brainstorming early ideas and methodologies with me and helping bring them to life.

A huge thanks to the brilliant author, super star speaker, and friend Sally Hogshead, who convinced me that I, too, could write a book and for connecting me to a number of individuals who helped to catapult me on the journey to bringing *Marketing in the Participation Age* to life.

I would like to thank the executive leadership team within ZenithOptimedia, specifically Tim Jones and Steve King, who are not afraid to embrace new ideas and are constantly reinventing to prepare for the future. Thanks also go to the amazing team at Performics who supported the idea, adopted the language, helped me get the project out the door, and continue to challenge my thinking every day. There is not a better performance marketing team in the world, and I am proud to work with you.

Finally, I would like to thank my mom for helping me hone my talent for expressing myself in writing, beginning at a very early age. I still believe I can do anything I set my mind to, and mostly that's because you told me from the beginning that I could.

INTRODUCTION

The Participation Age

The living room is quiet on Sunday morning, occupied only by a 17-year-old sitting in a gaming chair in front of the couch. He wears headphones to ensure he doesn't wake the rest of the family at such an early hour, and he is intently engrossed in game he is playing. Even though he is the only person sitting in the living room, he is not the sole participant engaged in this activity. Six thousand players from around the world are logged on this Sunday, even though it has, amazingly, been released for only a week. The game is Activision's Call of Duty: Black Ops. This participant happens to live in rural Idaho and doesn't know any of the other participants currently online. In fact, most of these participants have never met one another in person. But despite this fact, each has similar motivations for participating in Call of Duty: Black Ops. These reasons are not dissimilar from why individuals choose to take part in any activity—online or in the real world—such as a game, a physical sport, or even a political movement.

According to a report from research and education firm L2 Think Tank, more than 81 percent of upscale Gen Yers use the social media site Facebook every day. That's nearly twice the number of people who watch television or read newspaper content. Gen Yers are commonly defined as the technology-savvy generation, but what's more important and less commonly observed is the fact that Gen Yers were born participants. They have specific expectations about their relationships with peers, supervisors, and the companies whose products they use. They are masters at using the participation engine—or the Internet—via a number of devices. As Publicis Groupe, the third largest global communications company, chief strategy and innovation officer of VivaKi, Rishad Tobaccowala, explains, "The Internet was really the first addictive media following TV, and once someone experiences the Internet, their expectations change . . . dramatically." Reality has been altered in large part because of the connected devices we use to interact with the world. And it is now crucial that companies that operate in this new age understand the science behind participation and action.

Fortunately, the secret to unlocking participation is amazingly simple, because it's based on basic human needs and desires. Yes, the world is increasingly becoming digital, and the barrier between the real and the virtual world is becoming increasingly blurry. But deep down, and regardless of how much exposure we have to digital technology, people are still analog and very much human. The new participants are people who expect to work and live in environments that facilitate relationships and participation. People decide which products and services to purchase based on the enjoyment these bring to them, meaning they choose with their hearts, even though they may use technology to do the research and communicate and may use numbers to justify their choices.

The Participation Age is more fragmented, personal, and connected than we could ever have imagined—and it's always on and happening in real time. The Participation Age is about people who actively manage life by using the many technology tools available at their fingertips. Some research firms refer to this new era as the Customer Age, claiming that successful marketers in this new age will not simply focus on customers but be customer obsessed; others prefer to call them users, implying interaction is key. In either case, understanding customers in the form of simple demographics is no longer enough in a world where it's also no longer enough to simply broadcast a message and hope that people will receive it. Competitive companies understand that they must motivate customers to act on their behalf to be successful in the Participation Age.

Many organizations understand the importance of inspiring people to participate and of keeping them coming back. Gaming companies, for instance, have appreciated the value of participation for some time, for obvious reasons. Game development that is carefully paired with accompanying marketing techniques inspires participation that results in astoundingly repeatable bottom line results. Aforementioned gaming company Activision has been galvanizing participation for years—and enjoying phenomenal results for both player participation and financial rewards. In just 45 days following the November 9, 2010, release of Call of Duty: Black Ops, players logged more than 600 million hours of game participation. The total number of hours played is equivalent to more than 68,000 years, an average of 87 minutes per day per player. At the Call of Duty: Modern Warfare 3 launch in November 2011, Activision shipped an astonishing 6.5 million copies in just 24 hours, officially making it the largest entertainment launch in history. The $400 million in just one day of sales outpaced any box office gross, CD or book sales, or video game title in history. And these impressive numbers did not even include sales outside of the United States.

Participation has been integral to the video gaming industry's success, for obvious reasons. Without participants, there would be no Activision. Because it must, Activision actively acknowledges the value participants contribute to its brand. The company understands that harnessing participation will help it to edge out its competitors. As such, Activision's ingrained philosophy to succeed involves conscientiously planning every program—including marketing—to activate a set of interdependent motivational elements that work together to inspire someone to join, share, take part, play a role, connect, and engage. But in the Participation Age, motivating people to engage is critical to every brand, gaming company or not.

Determining what motivates people to engage is not a new area of study. Scholars, sociologists, and scientists across the ages—great minds like Aristotle, Sigmund Freud, Geoffrey Nunberg, and Abraham Maslow—have studied why people are intrinsically motivated. More recently, Edward Deci and Richard Ryan from the University of Rochester developed the self-determination theory in an effort to explain why humans are motivated to become involved in activities in a manner that results in enhanced performance, persistence, and creativity. The idea behind this theory is that individuals are intrinsically motivated to seek challenges and discover new perspectives—and in doing so, the activity itself stimulates their desire to actualize their individual human potential. If someone is intrinsically motivated, he or she will choose to actively engage and participate, and the experience will feel rewarding to that individual. These studies have prompted the definition of specific attributes that can be used to develop conditions for social environments that, when employed, facilitate and enable participation.

Self-determination theory has been applied to and is commonly used in fields ranging from psychology to education to health care to sports and exercise. It's also been used in the workplace as an employee retention and satisfaction tool. It has not been applied to marketing because it has not really been relevant to do so, since marketing as a discipline has traditionally been considered a passive activity. Until recently, it has consisted of a one-way persuasive message, broadcasted to an audience with the intent of changing perception and ultimately causing a behavior change that results in product demand. But over the past 10 years, every part of the product decision-making process began to involve individuals taking some form of action—and the behavior changes associated with this has only increased with mobile phone adoption. If someone wants to find out more information about a product or service, he or she can simply turn to the browser on his or her laptop, tablet, or phone or crowd-source an opinion from any social network. Technology has enabled participation in ways Aristotle never imagined.

According to the 2011 InSites Consulting Social Media Around the World Study, there are 7 billion people in the world, 2 billion Internet users, and 1 billion social network users. Of these, 600 million use their social networks at least daily, and 36 percent post company- or brand-related information. Besides the obvious desire to connect with others, getting information about new products and brands has increased social network membership, which only further illustrates that participants expect to have a relationship with the brands they use.

Never has there been a time more relevant for marketers to understand how to harness participation. Companies that focus on motivating individuals to participate with their brands will communicate more fluidly with customers and employees, add more value, and compete more effectively in today's connected world.

However, marketers are struggling to operate in the Participation Age because they are still using traditional marketing tools and philosophies developed originally for the broadcast mediums of radio and television. Perhaps even more fundamental is the fact that marketing in the Participation Age requires that marketers adopt a new philosophy and a new way of marketing altogether. This new philosophy begins with rethinking marketing basics. It's a mind-set shift in how companies and marketers view consumers and potential customers. Historically, marketing has been about informing an uninformed consumer—which is a rare thing in today's connected world. A more apt description of today's consumers would be sophisticated and informed participants who likely are more knowledgeable than the average retail salesperson and who have high expectations about their relationships with the brands they choose.

The transformation is fundamental, and because the behavior change requires that brands and marketing professionals conscientiously embrace a new mind-set and actions, I advocate starting with a language change. Words are an important first step in changing behavior. In this case, renaming consumers *participants* sparks a consciousness in marketers' minds that is instrumental in the new landscape—and it helps pave the way toward changing the processes and tools we use every day.

It is challenging to navigate the complex media environment and market to technology-savvy participants who expect a real-time relationship 24 hours a day, seven days a week. It no longer works to apply the old "send out a message and hope for the best" formula. And although most companies love the concept of embracing the notion of participation, the idea terrifies them somewhat, because there is no blueprint for marketing in the Participation Age.

The premise behind the Participation Way was to create a framework that is more than just another marketing tactic, big idea, viral program, or social media platform. In absence of a new approach—and in an effort to survive in today's complicated, fragmented, and dynamic media environment—many marketers are resorting to a defensive marketing approach. In essence, they're just continuing to react. Even though they are operating in a new environment, they still use the old linear marketing tools, formulas, and philosophies designed to persuade consumer opinions rather than invite them to participate in a relationship. These tools are perceived as good because they are thought to be controlled by the marketer, and they feel safe to many in a time when we worry that our choices might not be sound. And they were not designed to create and sustain reciprocal customer relationships in a marketplace driven by the participant where networks and relationships matter more than the message. Marketers are masters at persuasive message development, not at activating participation or engagement.

For the past five years, I have been working with clients struggling to work in the "flavor of the month" media environment: search, social, mobile, viral, and so on. In this complicated world, stressed marketing managers are doing what they have always done because it's familiar and perceived as tried and true, even though it no longer works. Yet there is a framework that brands can use to motivate participation. It's a formula I was seeking as a marketer working at Hewlett-Packard (HP), and it is a framework that my company currently uses to work with leading global brands that are striving to become revolutionists in the new marketing world. The Participation Way allows marketers to focus on a simple, new approach designed for motivating people to take action. It has been translated for marketing and provides a new language for the organization that can be used as the basis for training, planning, activating, and measuring marketing. For those brands that have embraced the concept, it has provided the foundation for a new type of dialogue within the organization, one of hope and inspiration that leads to clarity around action steps instead of the futile search for the next big idea. Let's get started!

1 Marketing in the Age of Participation

The moment it all crystallized for me stands out very clearly in my mind. It was early 2005, and I was still working in marketing at Hewlett-Packard (HP). I had to organize a meeting for a large global product launch for the Imaging and Printing Group and was specifically focused on helping the team develop launch plans for the United States. It had a significant digital marketing concept central to the big creative idea, which was something new. Big ideas, however, were not new; in fact, finding that magical big idea was the ultimate marketer's goal. The quest to uncover it usually began with a television concept that we would extend into the print and digital environments—if it worked. We had been counting on this formula for a number of years, and it had generally been a recipe for reasonable success.

But this time was different. The entire idea *itself* was about eliciting a response. The brilliant concept was designed to ignite participation from the individuals whom our message was trying to reach. This was not a "send out the message and see what happens" campaign. The idea itself was big, brilliant, and beautiful—but insufficient. In addition to the fact that we were asking for feedback, our audience actually had the tools to *take action*. This was significant, and that campaign suddenly made the notion of integration incredibly important.

Even before this campaign came about, I had acknowledged the growing challenges related to media interconnectedness. I understood how crucial integration was to achieve ultimate program effectiveness. Yet as important as it was, and as easy as it sounded, integration had suddenly become incredibly complex.

I was beginning to appreciate the challenges facing marketers in the new environment. The big idea, messages that had previously worked so well, were beginning to fail for several of reasons:

1. **Despite the fact that digital was—and is—outpacing all other mediums the television "big ideas" conquered all.** Even today, creative agencies are generally masters at crafting persuasive entertaining pieces designed for television, a medium meant for leaning back and being entertained. They usually don't even consider or invite audience participation. Ironically, in this case, the idea and tagline of the HP printing campaign was, "What do you have to say?"—which referred to the individual expression reflected in someone's printed piece. The tagline was a literal invitation for people to participate by building and printing individual creative pieces. HP invited participants to "say" something using creative units that didn't function well; they hadn't given much thought to how they would actually receive the "response" or engage in the dialogue. The harsh truth was we really didn't *want* them to tell us "what they had to say"; we just thought the tagline was a good way to articulate self-expression, something that generally resonated well with individuals using printers. As good creative agencies usually do, the big idea struck the central nervous system of a cultural theme a little ahead of its time. Customers really did want a "say" and wanted to participate. We just weren't prepared for the response, nor did we go about creating an environment that conscientiously fostered participation.

2. **Digital was the stepchild no one wanted to own and an afterthought.** Big creative agencies invested heavily in their creative and production talent in 2005. Their experience was in television and print. These agencies generally outsourced, often even contracting offshore, with small shops to create the web experience, that is, to do the actual coding for the ads or the sites,

usually as a way to save money. This meant that the end products sometimes didn't work correctly on the web and the concepts were never developed for the relationship medium. In addition, these other agencies usually built and managed other important digital cornerstones. The digital experience was built for creative units that were beautiful to the eye, meaning they were built in Flash and therefore invisible to search engines. So even if they *did* function properly and looked beautiful, no one could find them.

I discovered this the hard way—with a bit of a twist. Shortly before the campaign launch, we discovered that we had a poorly designed web experience and made the seemingly easy decision to hire another firm to take over. However, the coding was done in Portuguese and actually *finding* a firm with experience recoding Flash in that language was not as easy. We never would have outsourced the television component; we did this only with the digital assets, which firmly illustrated their priority and value in the marketing mix. And although this has changed somewhat today, it's not as much as one might expect given the importance of digital and search. According to the 2009 Global Interactive Marketing Organization and Agency Survey, most brand organizations have fewer than 10 employees working in digital. Despite the fact that digital mediums are growing, digital spend is still relatively small. In fact, a recent ZenithOptimedia ad forecast indicates that 95 percent of all future advertising growth will be on a screen (television and Internet). This study does not yet track mobile advertising growth, but it is projected to grow exponentially. This reinforces the importance of television and the increasing importance of interactive mediums.

3. **Media was an after-thought in the process.** And as I mentioned, it was frequently done by a different agency—and wasn't considered and involved until too late in the campaign process. Media innovation around the big idea had great potential, but

because the creative agency was the genesis of big ideas and consequently the owner of strategy and innovation, the media partner was brought in at the last moment for efficiency purposes. Any opportunities for further integration were subsequently lost. This, too, is improving today. In the 2012 Cannes Lions competition, the advertising industry's largest global annual awards show and festival for professionals in the creative communications industry, there were a number of creative entries in the media category and media entries in the creative categories. This is an indication that more campaigns—and certainly the best—are now effectively blending creative, media, and technology.

4. **All marketing assignments were designed as a form of persuasive entertainment.** This is the most fundamental reason for the impending failures. Marketers assumed that people were waiting to be entertained passively with a big idea that might influence an opinion—and that they were basically uninformed and required assistance in making a decision about a product or service. For decades, marketing's role was to aid people who simply needed information about a product in order to make a decision. This is where the idea of awareness originated. Programs were not designed to build a relationship with a person; we never asked ourselves what action we wanted them to take or thought of developing a two-way relationship. It never occurred to us to build programs fundamentally designed with participation in mind. And why should it have? Marketing tools, processes, and philosophies had developed and matured long before people used their computers, smartphones, or tablets to conduct an Internet search or ask their social network for feedback on a certain product or service.

On this particular day, I was working on integration planning. I began assembling a list of individuals and their respective agency partners who worked across multiple marketing disciplines required to launch the campaign. Individuals who managed their discipline needed to understand the other functional plans in order to see how the overall marketing program was connected. The more connected and integrated a program is, the stronger it becomes, especially in the new digital landscape. For example, paid search and organic search required coordination and integration for optimal effectiveness. Yet since *my* organization managed paid search, it was tied to advertising and marketing and therefore it was integrated with advertising flight schedules. The corporate information technology (IT) department managed organic search, and the campaign was not even on their radar. Nor did they consider it their role to integrate with the campaign at all. In general, search should be coordinated with direct marketing, which was managed by yet *another* group; with public relations; and so on. Somehow, all of these teams and their agencies had never even met one another until the day I brought them into the same meeting to discuss launch coordination and integration.

To plan the meeting, I had to track down individuals who managed various disciplines and identify their respective marketing partners. Eventually, the invitee list reached 60 people. How was I ever going to schedule a meeting for this many people? Even if I did get a reasonable attendance rate, how would we ever get through or plan the coordination in a way that both added value to individual functions and made the overall plan stronger? This was the moment that I realized that although we were operating using traditional marketing tools and processes, the world had changed. I knew that in order to plan, develop, and launch successful programs, marketing was due for an overhaul.

The meeting actually took place. I don't believe all 60 individuals made an appearance, although a number showed up in the room and others joined via phone. As each team discussed their individual plans and other teams asked questions, the overlap became very evident. In many cases, individual managers were not even asking the right questions about their individual programs, because they lacked information about other programs that ultimately affected their own. The tools, philosophies, processes, goals, and approaches—even the language around marketing—simply were not working any longer.

We have long known that big companies always have silos, and they're less than optimal at internal communications, which can often limit even seemingly obvious connections. Similar to any company, these teams were simply doing their jobs as they always had. The difference was *me*. I was no longer content with the "old" way. I struggled for a way to help others see the light, but I didn't have much success. The same conversations with the same words just occurred over and over again, which led to us using the same tools we had been using for years.

Words have always been important to marketers, who are masters at finding the right words, the right essence, and the right feeling to change perception. If you could change perception, then it was generally thought that a change in action would eventually follow. This is the core essence of any marketing brief: persuasive words that describe how one feels and how we want that person to feel after receiving our message. Marketers talk a lot about what we do and are doing to others. I was listening with a new ear, though, and suddenly it all seemed to have no meaning in the new world: *Above the line, below the line, big idea, marketing message, viral, reach, frequency, target, audience*— even *consumer*—I was just as guilty as everyone else, unconsciously using them over and over every day without really knowing what they meant or where they came from.

The marketing and media landscape in 2005 was decidedly less complex compared with today's highly networked complex environment. The rise of social media, the mobile explosion, and the fragmentation of media globally are increasing complexity.

Perhaps even more fundamental than the landscape in which we work in is the basic mind-set shift of the focus for *all* marketing efforts: the consumer. The evolution of consumer sophistication and expectations is demanding a change in our marketing fundamentals, more so than any other single factor. Having lived or been born with technology tools that arm them with a constant supply of information, today's consumers now have new expectations about their relationships with the brands whose products and services they use. They have evolved well beyond the uninformed, passive, undecided individuals they once were. They are new participants who expect to join, connect, share, take part, and engage with other people and brands. They believe that their voice makes a difference—and they're right.

Because I worked for a big global company on a market-leading product line, I had the privilege of working with brilliant agencies to architect beautiful creative masterpieces. These were mostly big ideas designed first for television and intended to wow consumers into finding out more about something they were unaware of. Although these concepts were stunningly elegant and beautiful, they often didn't translate well in the interactive environment—because they were not *designed* for the participative environment. We never asked the question, What action do you want someone to take when he or she sees this? That is, until the "What do you have to say?" campaign came about. Suddenly, we *were* asking them to take an action and *do* something. We weren't prepared for the response, but the new participant was expecting more than a response. They were expecting a reciprocal *relationship*.

The decades of marketing in one-way communication messages were gone. This realization suddenly led to my desire to find out how we got here to begin with—and set out to understand more about the history of marketing before beginning the journey into marketing for the future.

Participant Marketing Summary

1. The controlled and linear tools, processes, and philosophies we use for marketing were developed for a different era in marketing, not today's Participation Age.

2. Most marketing ideas have been generated by creative shops that are masters at crafting persuasive and entertaining pieces designed for television, a medium meant for leaning back and being entertained. They rarely consider formulating ideas around inviting audience participation.

3. Media is generally an afterthought in the process—an approach that is not conducive to the dynamic and complex media environment we live in today.

4. Inviting action and tracking performance are on most marketer wish lists, but they are often difficult to implement.

5. It's nearly impossible to deliver truly integrated marketing in today's fragmented and complex media environment, and it's increasingly difficult for marketers to control this delivery.

6. Many marketers are not even aware of *why* they are using the language, tools, and processes they use every day, but they always have and continue to do so because it feels safe and there are few alternatives.

2 The Catalyst

The Consumer-to-Participant Transformation

*We are what we repeatedly do. Excellence, then, is not an act,
but a habit.*

—Aristotle

Ironically, the process of starting a revolution often begins very simply with a focus on words. Marketers have habits that have been around for more than 50 years, and we have become accustomed to using words as powerful tools in our trade. This began with copywriting. Although I'm merely midway into my second decade of marketing career, I do sometimes consider how much and how little has changed when I watch episodes of AMC's *Mad Men*, a television series about one of New York's most prestigious ad agencies at the beginning of the 1960s.

The purpose in creating change is not just to do something once; it's about repetitive transformation. When I parted ways with Hewlett-Packard (HP) in 2006, I was eager to set off a marketing revolution, and that meant creating a process for the new world of marketing that could stand the test of time. Humans are creatures of repetition, something that became incredibly evident as I learned more and more about marketing. All of us can identify with the idea of short-lived motivation.

Many people start out with a goal and quit within a few weeks. Once the motivation dies down, their actions cease. Of course, they won't get the desired results once they stop taking action. To become successful and obtain the goals you have set for yourself or your company, you must take the necessary actions to make it a habit. The first lesson I learned in revolutionizing marketing is that it's not easy. The truth is, old habits are hard to break.

A focus on words seems appropriate for participant marketing given the fact that conversational media has become mainstream. If the medium is about conversations, then words matter. Language might seem minute in the scheme of things, but words have always been foundational components to any marketing program. And since

I realized how difficult these habits would be to break, I recognized the need to create something that would cause people to stop and think. Sometimes a simple word change can serve as a reminder that behavior change needs to follow. It's a nudge that makes us pause, analyze our actions, and recognize a window of opportunity for change. The word I settled on is one that marketers use dozens of time a day, and ironically, it's the word that all the fuss is about in marketing to begin with: *consumer*.

I did a great deal of listening during the early days of my research for this book. I listened to conversations in meetings at HP and to agency and industry leaders and marketers from other companies as they discussed the new challenges in the space. I attended an industry conference in Park City, Utah, and listened for two days as leading marketers from agency, client, and publisher companies talked with frustration about how the world had changed and argued about new ways to approach marketing. I attended an ad:tech conference session during which I closed my eyes and listened to panel members use the same words 10 or 20 times. The words here aren't the issue; however, the word *consumer* is poignant to a world that no longer really exists. It made me think long and hard about a word I had used multiple times a day for over 20 years. Where did the word come from? Is it still relevant? Does it really matter? I asked all of these questions because I was interested in proposing a fundamental change. In the end, I took the leap, and that decision paved the path for developing new tools and processes. Deciding to make the radical change of dropping the word *consumer* and adopting *participant* is about an internal rallying cry to change everything about marketing.

Although my instincts led me down the participant-driven marketing path, I decided to research marketing in general to affirm or challenge the new lexicon. The journey not only affirmed my decision but helped me understand how we got here in the first place—and why the basic principles of marketing were created. I also encountered many marketers who also lacked the context and history.

Most marketers I know have been able to experience a look back to the roots of our industry thanks to AMC's popular hit series. The era depicted in *Mad Men* was a groundbreaking time for the advertising industry. Radio had an impact on agencies and marketers, but when television became mainstream, it revolutionized our industry— not unlike what the Internet triggered more recently. In fact, it was during the broadcast revolution when nearly all the tools and language we use today were introduced as new and avant-garde.

The notion of consumerism is decades older than the 1960s era of *Mad Men*, and it isn't an original American or even an advertising notion. To understand that we must take another 40-year step back and begin where the conversation should begin in participant marketing: with the *participant*—or, in this case, the evolutionary precursor to the participant, the consumer.

I have no idea how many times I've used the word *consumer* in the 20-something years I've been a marketer. There was at least a decade during my career when I considered myself a "consumer advocate" inside my company and even my industry—because I thought it was what responsible marketers should do. After all, it is easy for marketers to lose sight of the consumers' needs or point of view when their sole goal is to persuade a group of individuals to buy into the product or service they represent. I thought that being a consumer advocate made me better at what I did—and even helped product marketing create better products. I truly thought being a consumer champion would benefit the consumer at the same time it benefitted the company I represented, at least as much as one can as a biased marketer.

Yet I never stopped to consider where the term *consumer* actually came from. What does it mean to be a consumer? What is consumerism? What is a consumer product, other than the product an individual and not a business purchases? I believed then, and still do, that truly understanding consumer needs and their underlying roots are important to developing effective marketing materials. I have also strongly held that customer-brand relationships are crucial, which meant to me that the holistic consumer relationship could not solely be marketing's responsibility. This is a challenge in the traditional corporate structure where teams are organized in silos for scale and efficiency purposes. The reality is that the silo approach to creating, marketing, distributing, and supporting products had all worked relatively well for a long, long time. All these departments had a role in assisting product launches in some way. The consumer was just a by-product of this process. Messaging was a proven effective market-ing method to sell products—until digital came along and provided consumers tools and subsequently changed expectations.

Peter N. Stearns, provost and professor of history at George Mason University, defines *consumerism* as "a society in which many people formulate their goals in life partly through acquiring goods that they clearly do not need for subsistence or for traditional dis-play." His definition of a *consumer product* is "any product not required for basic sustenance."

Stearns claims that until recently, it was thought that con-sumerism was of American origin, a product of the US Industrial Revolution that developed at the turn of the nineteenth century. Plenty of fingers have been pointed at the United States for all things consumerism, both good and bad. It's been the only in last decade that historians declared this theory incorrect, letting people know that consumerism, in fact, first originated in eighteenth-century Western Europe and spread to the United States later.

Interestingly, one of the products that fascinated people enough to cause consumer behavior very early on was sugar. Although sugar did not in and of itself represent all the characteristics of consumer-ism as we define it today, it did suggest a "taste" for something that was by no means required for everyday survival. There are recorded instances of other consumer-like behaviors occurring around the same time—spending on household furnishings and decorative items, products that by definition were *not* required to remain alive.

The tulip is another relatively well-known example of recorded early consumer behavior. Initially imported from Turkey in the sixteenth century, tulips became so popular in 1630s Holland that market demand caused bulb prices to skyrocket. I, like many other people, always thought tulips originated in Holland; even today's tulip companies capitalize on this perception. Do a quick Google search for tulip bulbs, and you'll see the Holland windmill–decorated site for Breck listed as the top or near top paid result. Their tagline is still "Bulbs from Holland since 1818."

In 1600, tulips had no basic needs function. They could not be eaten or used for medicinal purposes. The attraction to the unique flower originally arose from a desire of individuals who wanted to display their power and status, which they thought the tulip could do because of its popularity with the Holland royal family. As a result, the tulip became a novelty item in mid-seventeenth-century Holland. By the 1640s, speculators were trading on future tulip consumption. People weren't seeking only the flowers themselves; paintings of tulips and other flowers also blossomed (no pun intended!) during this time.

Tulip consumption had a significant negative impact on Holland's economy, and this event is considered by many to be the first recorded economic bubble in history. Holland's tulip craze is thought to be a first glimpse of future consumer behavior. Clearly, tulips were not a basic need product, yet demand nearly bankrupted the Dutch economy. It is also an example of consumerism thriving before World War II outside of the United States. Because of their cost, tulips were not widely available to ordinary people. No similar fad product replaced the tulip after the bubble; however, sugar and tulips have become signatures of early consumer society behavior.

Another consumerism signature European development during this time frame was the evolution of peddlers and market fairs, which were considered the first retail shops. With shops came shoppers and all the early precursors to the things we know and love about the retail experience today.

Soon enough, European colonies populated what would become the United States and brought these practices with them. Consumer society gained momentum in the United States at the turn of the twentieth century. Novelist Virginia Woolf wrote in 1910 about how Americans were changing the nature of human character. In the 1920s, journalist Samuel Strauss suggested the term *consumptionism* to characterize this new way of life that, he said, "created a person with a philosophy that committed human beings to the production of more and more things and emphasized standard of living" above all other values. Although the Industrial Revolution did not cause consumerism—or government concern for the economy, along with the spread of department stores and even public relations and advertising— it certainly contributed to the rapid rate of development.

According to William Leach in his book titled *Land of Desire: Merchants, Power, and the Rise of a New American Culture*, published in 1993, the production of goods in America from the mid-1800s to 1930 is a demonstration of the rate and level of commodity consumption. Food production grew by nearly 40 percent from 1899 to 1905; the production of ready-to-wear clothing and costume jewelry doubled between 1890 and 1900; and glassware and lamp production went from 84,000 tons in 1890 to 250,563 tons in 1914. In 1890, 32,000 pianos were sold in the United States; by 1904, the number sold increased to 374,000.

Leach goes on to describe that during this period, the perfume industry, unquestionably not a product required for a society focused on the necessities of everyday sustenance, became the country's 10th largest industry. At one department store, sales of toiletries rose from

$84,000 to $522,000 between 1914 and 1926. The manufacture of clocks and watches increased almost two and a half times, increasing from 34 million to 82 million in just 10 years. By the late 1920s, one of every six Americans owned an automobile.

Manufacturing and production in the early twentieth century is relevant because it marked the early phase of what British-Czech philosopher and social anthropologist Ernest Gellner called the "society of perpetual growth." It also marked the creation of a new type of culture: consumer capitalism—along with the construction of a new type of person: the consumer.

Around this same time, two other categories of industry emerged: the capitalist and the laborer. Of course, merchants had existed for thousands of years—even before retailers—and people had always labored to produce goods and consumed what they produced, even in a nonproduction environment. What is perhaps most thought provoking and least known among today's marketers is that capitalism and consumerism did not exist until the 1920s. The sole purpose of the consumer was to purchase and *consume* increasing quantities of goods and services as industries increased efficiency and overproduced products.

As early as the late 1890s, technological advances helped enhance production processes. This caused such a substantial increase in the goods produced that government officials feared overproduction, panic, and the severe economic depression that marked that decade. Out of these fears came what William Leach called "a steady stream of enticements" designed to "entice people to consume and save them from making inappropriate choices."

The birth of advertising is closely related to the consumerism in the United States. Businesses required efficient ways to produce these enticements for consumers, whose role was necessary to save the capitalists from their own efficiency. Consumers required advertisers to "save them" from making inappropriate choices and provide information about products and services they didn't know about. World War I reinforced the growth of consumerism and the advertising industry as well; as the government made a concentrated effort to set the country back on its feet and put people back to work, it strongly urged citizens to buy products from businesses that hired returning war veterans. As General Motors' Charles Kettering wrote in his 1929 article for *Nation's Business* titled "Keep the Consumer Dissatisfied," "The key to economic prosperity is the organised creation of dissatisfaction." This is all a fitting birth to the era depicted in *Mad Men*—an era of shining knights whose role was it was to save the day by helping unaware consumers make emotional decisions about products and services.

Of course, it wasn't just the advertising industry's responsibility to guide consumers. Public relations also played a role, and the rise of consumerism in the United States is also linked to the birth of public relations. In 1915, Edward Bernays, often cited as the father of public relations, created World War I propaganda techniques for the US government designed to influence public opinion about the war. Bernays helped the government gain substantial support in wartime; once the war had ended, he began to apply his knowledge in the areas of business and commerce. One of his famous expressions is, "The conscious and intelligent manipulation of the opinions of the masses is an important element in a democratic society. It is the intelligent minorities which need to make use of propaganda continuously and systematically." If only Bernays could see a world in which we strategically monitor and gain insight from the "opinions of the masses" collected from an invisible, massive network in our complex, connected, and participative world today.

Every day, even multiple times a day, we use the words *consumer*, *audience*, and *target* to describe the individual or group or groups of individuals with whom we desire to connect. These people, or groups of people, are the most important consideration of any marketing program. After all, the program is being created *for* them so they are inspired, persuaded, and then take action. Yet, are these the words we would use to accurately describe someone we respect and with whom we want to have a relationship? Do we even know where these words originated? Or are we using them simply because they're familiar and comfortable?

Sit around for just 10 minutes at any marketing trade show and close your eyes to focus. Just listen. Listen to the language being used even today in your organization or at an industry event. *Consumer, target*, and *audience* are spoken numerous times in nearly every presentation or conversation—along with *reach, frequency*, and other familiar phrases such as *above the line* and *marketing funnel*, to name a few.

I have asked a number of experienced marketing individuals if they know where the words or phrases came from or what they mean, and many have never thought about the definitions. To be honest, I didn't know the meaning or the origin of many before I set out on this journey. Some we know as marketers, but some we don't. Either way, it seems as though this vocabulary has been forever part of our marketing way of life; we use the words and phrases because they are what we know. But these words and phrases are at best inaccurate or out of date in a participation culture. And at worst, they are derogatory, insensitive, or even insulting.

There is an awakening occurring among yesterday's consumers—today's participants. Unquestionably, negative implications of being labeled "consumers" are washing over more people than just marketers today. *Washington Post* columnist Michelle Singletary wrote an article on January 4, 2009, emphasizing this point quite clearly: "One of my New Year's resolutions is to stop referring to myself as a consumer." The idea for the resolution actually came from reader Tom Krohn, who suggested that "it's not just the country's spending habits that need to change for the better but the language we use to describe who we are." Singletary went on to discuss the transformation from consumption culture to participation culture: "We use the word consumer interchangeably when referring to ourselves even when the topic isn't about consuming. But look at the word consume. According to the Merriam-Webster dictionary, consume means 'to do away with completely; destroy, to spend wastefully; squander.' And yet we are no longer citizens but consumers. The recession has proved that things have to change, and still the message from many of our leaders continues to be that consumerism—consumers—will save the day. To be a consumer is equivalent to being a good American."

There has been a certain amount of consumer backlash for a long time, and I am not advocating an anticonsumer movement in the broad sense. Anticonsumer activists define *consumerism* as something more than benign consumption. For thousands of years, humans have consumed items that they did not manufacture or gather themselves—in other words, things that were made by other people that they didn't really *need*. The negative sentiment surrounding consumerism emerged in the late nineteenth and early twentieth centuries, when Americans—and citizens of other industrial nations—began buying most of what they consumed, rather than producing it at home. Anticonsumer activists take issue with the assumption that consumerism is somehow a natural human urge. They further argue that the values that came about in a hierarchical system where mass production, communication, and urbanization rendered older values less relevant to the national experience is dysfunctional. The television shows that address hoarding and show consumers who are obsessed with collecting unnecessary items has brought attention to the subject recently as well.

Participant marketing does not support an anticonsumer movement. It simply encourages marketing professionals to consciously recognize that we are now operating in a new era: the Participation Age. And this new environment requires new language. The change begins with a conscious choice to replace the word *consumer* with *participant*—along with making other vocabulary changes. This will help initiate a marketing revolution that activates a different mind-set. If the participant thrives in a challenging, empowered environment supported by an approach to which he or she can relate, then it's our responsibility as marketers to create a relationship and environment that nurtures this participative culture. New words help us think about changing our processes, which, in turn, will help us change our behavior.

If consumers are now participants who are actively engaged in their environments, then the word *audience* is similarly imprecise. I know for a fact that people are not sitting on the edge of their seats, waiting for a television commercial to air or looking for the next advertisement in a magazine as they turn the page. I am reminded of this every evening as I avoid the ads using the remote control on my digital video recorder. In the early days of television, when the media landscape was uncluttered and technology required captive spectators, the audience analogy was appropriate, as viewers sat in front of their televisions or radios each evening waiting to be entertained.

It is estimated that an advertiser in 1960 could invest in three television ads and reach more than 80 percent of the individuals in the marketplace. And, because the media landscape was sparse, the marketer's sole job was to convey information about the product to an individual. It truly was a case of "tell them, and they will come." Studies proved that if a marketer could reach an individual with a brand message three times, consumers would then take action and ultimately sales would occur. It was upon this science that media models were built.

Henry Jenkins, provost's professor of communication, journalism, and cinematic arts at the University of Southern California, has written consistently and frequently about participation. Jenkins, who was formerly part of the MIT Media Lab, has also penned a number of books about media and culture. His book *Convergence Culture*, published in 2006, describes *convergence culture* as not primarily as a technological revolution but rather a cultural shift that depends on consumers' active participation working in a social dynamic. In a more recent blog post dated February 11, 2009, Jenkins focused on rethinking the old marketing labels: "So does it make sense any more to speak about media audiences or, for that matter, consumers in this brave new world of spreadable media? Probably not." He then goes on to describe other experts who have offered up new labels for the people formerly known as the audience, including *loyals, prosumers, inspirational consumers, connectors*, and *influencers*. Jenkins's eight-part blog series is part of a white paper developed in 2010 by his Convergence Culture Consortium on the topic of what he calls "spreadable media." Jenkins is an excellent example of the dialogue happening in marketing circles today. Whatever it's called, spreadable media, social media, and digital media are the new processes and tools required for participant marketing.

As I mentioned before, marketers have always valued *words*. Even before television copywriters identified emotional words to describe products or services, they understood that they needed to tap into emotional attributes to influence someone. That said, however, we are not very specific about the words we chose within our industry to describe what *we* do. If consumers are active participants with whom marketers must develop an ongoing relationship, then one of the most derogatory terms in our language has to be the word *viral* and its associated meaning. It's both imprecise and disparaging.

In the imprecision category, the term has *viral* has been used to describe so many related but ultimately distinct practices, ranging from word-of-mouth marketing programs to video mashups, social media applications, and videos posted to YouTube. Yet what is considered as *viral* is simply unclear. It is invoked in discussions about buzz marketing and brand building, and it also appears in conversations about direct marketing, social networks, and social marketing, as well as word-of-mouth and event marketing (which may not relate to online activities at all). It is generally assumed that it means something that spreads quickly like a contagious outbreak, affecting large numbers of individuals across virtual and real-world networks. The concept of viral distribution is meaningful for understanding in the participatory landscape. Ultimately, however, the viral metaphor is a flawed concept—and, I would argue, even a disparaging way to describe content distribution in a participant-driven environment.

When we refer to active sharing of content as viral, we recognize only the original idea creator. Sometimes the creator is a marketer or brand. Sometimes the creator is an individual or participant. In either case, use of the term *viral* fails to consider what actually happens in the participatory culture of communication in which ideas become augmented as they pass from participant to participant. Furthermore, participants make an active choice to actually distribute the information. It is a bit arrogant to imply that someone has had such an ingenious idea that the transmission is involuntary, that participants are "unknowingly infected" with something that becomes an epidemic. Professor Jenkins discussed the biological metaphor to describing participant media by saying, "The metaphor of 'infection' reduces consumers to the involuntary 'hosts' of media viruses, while holding onto the idea that media producers can design 'killer' texts which can ensure circulation by being injected directly into the cultural 'bloodstream.'"

In reality, this is not at all representative of what occurs. As we begin to discuss intrinsic motivation and nurturing participation, it is essential to remember that all *brands* are participants, too. They are content creators that have a voice, a point of view, and contribution in communities. In the Participation Age, all participants, including brands, are created equal. Believing that we somehow control the big idea or creative concept and that if we are good at our craft we can cause something to become viral by planting this wonderful idea in the right place boosts our marketing egos. However, this belief perpetuates advertisers' and media producers' inflated sense of power—their belief that they can shape the communication process and manipulate the messaging. Ironically, they *desire* a viral program because they believe it is creates free media that acquires a large reach without having to spend as much, which may or may not be true. There is also something mystical and magical about creating something viral, because it's not well understood. In either case, this rarely happens in a controlled manner that preserves the message's purity or the quality of the reach.

Given these limitations, I propose a substitute for *viral:* participant media and amplification. The participant approach embraces the empowered participant's role in "amplifying" media content. And in doing so, it often expands opportunities and unlocks brand opportunities with unanticipated new customers, introduces new ideas, and even potentially helps produce new creative concepts. If a brand is brave enough to allow participants to add value, then it may become more meaningful to those encountering the message. This also perpetuates the notion of a "spiral" by encouraging others to add value and pass on the content; hence, the marketer's goal becomes keeping the participation spiral spinning.

Again, there are some very important points to keep in mind about the language we choose as we embark on a marketing program. If marketers are looking for something viral, then they lose the opportunity to invite others to participate with a tried-and-true approach right from the beginning. This viral method makes it much more difficult to encourage individuals to take part by utilizing the Participation Way, a new marketing philosophy and approach developed for the Participation Age.

I recently attended an industry panel discussion titled "How to Create Successful Viral Marketing Programs" that began with each member sharing his or her definition of the word *viral*. It progressed to a conversation about how to create something viral for marketing purposes. Each panel member cited one or two programs he or she considered to be an example of a viral marketing program. One panelist began by suggesting that a viral marketing campaign was one "where the creative concept was compelling enough that it spread through social channels in a matter of days." This suggests that we need to hire great creative shops that understand how to develop viruses that work on social networks. Of course, this was probably due to the fact that this individual just happened to work for a company who claimed to have experience creating brilliant viral ideas. Another panelist described a viral campaign as something he would find cool enough to pass on to his own friends. Another panel member, also a content creator, described viral as purely a video concept. You can likely guess that she ran a very popular video start-up. Only one thing was clear at the close of the panel: there really wasn't a clear philosophy or predictable model for creating viral content or how to measure it, beyond reach or speed of reach.

What if, instead, at the onset of a business challenge, marketers developed *all* marketing programs to be participatory, thereby employing a known framework for inspiring participation? What if brands viewed themselves as content creators? What if they took this into account from the program's inception and invited feedback throughout the process to continually improve the program and approach marketing as participants themselves? The panel discussion would be much more fruitful—and likely to provide a common framework for success—if everyone understood the intent and desired outcome.

Douglas Rushkoff's 1994 book *Media Virus* may not have originally coined the term *viral*, but he describes the media virus as a "Trojan horse that surreptitiously brings messages into our homes—messages can be encoded into a form people are compelled to pass along and share, allowing the embedded meanings, buried inside like

DNA, to 'infect' and spread, like a pathogen." This sounds like a viral program to me. I believe there is an integral part of our marketing DNA that really is fond of the idea that we are *so* clever that we can create something so compelling that our marketing campaign and messages spread without the participants' consent. We want to think that we can prompt people to take action without understanding the true intent. Yet we know that's not what happens today if we look deeply. And I'd like to save us from our own egotistical view. Any form of participant media requires a *conscious* action on the part of the *participant*.

Our confidence in our marketing abilities is also what makes us good at what we do—as long as we remember the context of the environment in which we operate and that it's vastly different than what it has been.

We have all have experienced what it's like to be part of a viral experience. Jokes, YouTube videos passed on from a friend via Facebook, and so on; we have an intense desire to share it with our own networks, and in doing so, we experience being part of something larger. Humans are social creatures who truly enjoy participation. We are deeply wired to share and participate, network, and connect with other humans. It gives us great satisfaction to somehow belong to something much larger. I have often typed a text message into my phone and marveled at the thought of how many other thousands of individuals might be typing the same word or phrases into their phones at the same time. The amount of inconsequential and seemingly fragmented and aggregated information that we encounter each day may actually have significant impact on our belief and actions. Marketing in the Participation Age demands that brands focus on motivating participants to join, share, take part, and connect—and changing the language we use is the first step. The next step is to understand the media landscape we live in today, as well as the media terms and philosophies. Once again, this requires a look back in history.

Participant Marketing Summary

1. The word *consumer* is not an accurate description of the highly networked, interactive, and reciprocal environment of the Participation Age. Participants are masters at using the participation engine, that is, the Internet. A consumer requires assistance to make informed choices; participants do not.

2. How often do you use the following words or phrases in your marketing practice? *Consumer, above the line, below the line, target, marketing funnel, four Ps* (product, price, promotion, place), *reach, frequency, audience, viral,* and *earned or nonearned media.*

3. The birth of advertising is closely related to the birth of consumerism, both of which were bolstered by World War I. The government at this time made a concentrated effort to get the country back to work and strongly urged citizens to buy products and services from companies that hired returning veterans.

4. Participant marketing encourages marketers to consciously recognize that we are now in the Participation Age, where participants make an active choice to create and distribute content.

5. Everyone, including brands, is now a participant and a content creator with a voice, a point of view, and a contribution to make to the community.

6. *Participant media* and *amplification* are more accurate words to describe what is often called a viral phenomenon.

3 Tools for the Past 60 Years

Mad Men character Don Draper sits in a Midtown Manhattan office of the fictional agency Sterling Cooper Draper Pryce in the 1960s. The *Mad Men* advertisers were master persuaders, epitomized by Don Draper, who is a creative genius surrounded by mystique. Advertising as a concept wasn't a new phenomenon in the 1960s. The first advertising agencies actually launched in the United States in the 1870s, followed by the first French agency in 1922. The industry then grew at a steady rate after World War I.

The introduction of broadcast media was the last big evolution of our industry prior to the Internet, and radio was the first widespread mass medium. By the end of World War II, 95 percent of all homes had radios, but television already had begun to erode its popularity by the early 1950s. As a result, radio stations began to shift their programming focus from news and story segments to music. The transistor radio positively affected radio growth by allowing for the production of cheap, portable radios that people could use in cars or outdoors. Interestingly, a large number of "hackers" who assembled radios at home using spare parts also helped spread radio accessibility.

During radio's golden age, advertisers sponsored entire programs, usually with some sort of message such as, "We thank our sponsors for making this program possible," that aired at the beginning or end of a program. During this time period, it was certainly appropriate to create an advertisement for an audience, as Americans gathered around their sets each evening to listen to their favorite shows. Although radio had the obvious limitation of being restricted to sound and took cues from earlier print advertising copywriting, larger stations began to experiment with different formats, primarily sound effects, as the industry developed.

Television technology was actually developed before commercial radio. As had happened with the spread of radio, hackers also built homegrown televisions, even though commercially built sets only slowly gained traction. By the end of the 1920s, the United States had 15 experimental television stations. On the eve of World War II, RCA, a pioneer in the industry, introduced television standards for production purposes. In response, the National Television System Committee, created by the Federal Communications Commission (FCC), developed recommendations for electronic television system submitted standards that were adopted in 1941. World War II delayed the commercial development of the television, and by the end of the war, fewer than 7,000 working television sets existed in the United States, and only nine stations were actually on the air. The United States was the leader in television technology, primarily because advances were made directly before, during, and after World War II, when America's major competitors in television development, Germany and England, halted their research programs due to the distraction of war.

The earliest television networks in the United States (NBC, CBS, ABC, and DuMont) were actually part of the larger radio network systems, and many early television shows were simulcasts of popular radio shows. In 1951, ABC merged with United Paramount Theaters and gained size and resources as a result. DuMont was unable to survive and by 1956 was no longer in business, with ABC having assumed many of DuMont affiliate stations. Networks offered centralized sales, distribution, and production services, which lowered costs for individual affiliates. This system was geared toward generating advertising revenue as well, because advertisers were interested in the ability to reach nationwide audiences.

During the first half of the 1950s, televisions sales proliferated, not dissimilar to the rise of personal computers, Internet adoption, and today's mobile phone adoption. Although only 0.5 percent of US households had a television set in 1946, more than 55 percent had one in 1954, and 90 percent had one by 1962. This had a negative impact on other public forms of entertainment, including the closing of movie theaters as motion pictures competed with television for attention.

What is interesting here is not a thesis or history lesson on television in America but that it is similar to the rise of the Internet. The Internet was also first embraced by hackers and dismissed, much like television was initially. Due to the steady rise of all digital media today, traditional forms of media are suffering as a consequence. In 2010, after 305 years, newspaper advertising revenue has been surpassed by the Internet; it had already been long eclipsed by television. We sometimes think that what is happening to us in the digital revolution is new and unique—and in some respects, this is true. However, there are similarities, and because nearly all of our marketing tools and processes were built for broadcast mediums, it's helpful to have context and understanding of the broadcast era.

There is a debate over when the first television advertisement was broadcast in the United States. Some sources claim it occurred on July 1, 1941, when watchmaker Bulova paid nine dollars for a placement on New York station WNBT before a Brooklyn Dodgers versus Philadelphia Phillies baseball game. It was a 20-second spot that displayed a picture of a clock superimposed on a map of the United States, accompanied by the voice-over "America runs on Bulova time." Incidentally, Bulova also claims to be the first company to produce the nation's first radio commercial: "At the tone, it's eight PM, B-U-L-O-V-A, Bulova watch time."

Over the next 15 years, the marketing philosophy, process, and approach as we know it today began to take shape. The advertising men of the 1950s and 1960s were investing time and money into conducting studies and surveys to measure advertising effectiveness and were building advertisements for radio and television. One outcome of this research prompted a decision to create shows that featured a single product or a line of products from a single company. Resembling radio show sponsorship of the past, sponsors were affiliated with specific shows, such as the *Kraft Television Theatre, Colgate Comedy Hour*, and *Coke Time*. Consumer packaged good companies were large advertisers, and it's likely no coincidence that this form of advertising was designed for companies with large families of products.

This strategy seemed effective for the marketers until television gained more popularity and there were more people watching programming. In an effort to generate more profit, networks began raising the sponsorship costs based on the number of people they claimed the shows were reaching. Costs associated with producing new content were also rising at this time, so networks created a new approach for developing advertising. This was named for and heavily leveraged from "magazine concept" advertising, or as we know it today, minute blocks of time during a show. NBC executive Sylvester L. "Pat" Weaver is credited with creating the magazine concept wherein sponsors would purchase blocks of time (typically 1 to 2 minutes) in a show, rather than sponsor an entire show. This would allow the network to book a variety of sponsors—a maximum of four was the original number proposed—for a show.

This was a significant development, as networks would now control the programming content because no one advertiser would "own" a particular show. It's ironic to think this idea came from the print model of advertising, although not so ironic if we consider it in a historical context. It's natural human behavior to start with what we know and adapt. This is clearly the pattern we are still following today as advertising evolves from broadcast to digital. Through the evolution of broadcast media, packaged goods companies once again led the way in pioneering this new form of advertising, including Procter & Gamble with such disparate products as Tide, Crest, and Jif.

The multiple spot per show dominated television advertising by 1960, and it has ever since. Instead of relying on audience identification with a specific show, sponsors now spread their messages across the schedule in an effort to reach as many consumers as possible. This approach proved to be very effective for the sponsors. Instead of being locked into a specific time block on a particular network every day or every week, sponsors could now choose the times and networks to display their message.

Nearly all of our marketing tools and processes were founded during this time. They were based on the assumption that companies could acquire customers in two ways: (1) through retail contact or word of mouth or (2) via broad-based media awareness. This is a very linear and logical approach to marketing. Make enough people aware of the product or service by providing them with a persuasive message enough times, and they'll take some type of action. It is what was, and often still is, taught in academic institutions, and all marketing principles fall from the assumption. The scientific basis for marketers' decisions was based on the mathematics applied to the media formula and the science around the compelling and persuasive message. We will focus on the science around the compelling message in the planning chapter.

Reach is an important discussion point for now, however, because we are still using it as a basis for planning marketing programs. The actual definition of *reach* is the total number of individuals or households exposed to the advertisement, at least once, during a given period of time. Reach may be stated either as an absolute number or as a fraction of a given population (for instance, it may be defined as TV households, men, or those aged 25 to 35). Any given viewer has been "reached" by the ad if he or she has viewed it (in its entirety or a specified amount) during the specified period. Multiple viewings by a single individual in the time period do not increase reach; however, media people use the term *effective reach* to describe the quality of exposure.

Effective reach and reach are two different measurements for a target audience who receives a given message or ad. Reach proved to be an effective way to market goods and services—and one reason for this was the limitation of the media landscape itself. An advertiser in the 1960s could run one television commercial during prime time on three different channels and reach 85 percent of the viewing audience, whereas today's advertiser would have to run the commercial more than 125 times during the same period to reach 85 percent of the viewing audience. Furthermore, advertisers 50 years ago did not have to worry about their viewers using digital video recorders (DVRs) to skip their ads completely as they do today. More than 50 percent of viewers today have either TiVos or DVRs. This technology has clearly changed the way people watch television—and has actually made it so that some viewers may not watch the advertising at all.

TiVos and DVRs are a mixed blessing to the television industry. These devices allow viewers to watch shows they might have otherwise missed. This, along with the number of portable devices enabled for viewing, are increasing the overall time spent watching television. However, when viewers use the machines to watch shows, they may often skip over commercials. This is obviously a painful fact for advertisers, who consider commercials an important part of their marketing investment, and for the networks, which need the money to produce shows. It's also interesting to note that a number of recent studies indicate that more than 50 percent of television viewers watch television while simultaneously interacting with a tablet, notebook, or mobile phone. It's likely that television viewing will continue to rise, but unlike the traditional media habits, this is not an "either-or" choice for the marketer trying to reach viewers. Participants have now demonstrated the capability to be passive *and* active at the same time. This is another indication of the growing complexity in the new media landscape.

Marketing was a one-way form of communication in this former era of advertising, because most advertising innovation was based on print, radio, and television. The idea was—and still is—to broadcast a television commercial to millions of viewers and replay it enough times that it eventually causes the viewers to take some form of action. We actually believe it causes action because of something called *frequency theory*. This notion is based primarily on research conducted by Herbert E. Krugman, who authored "The Impact of Television Advertising: Learning without Involvement" in 1965 while he was employed at General Electric.

According to Krugman, there were only three levels of exposure in psychological terms: curiosity, recognition, and decision. Krugman's frequency theory has been adopted and widely used in advertising for decades. Many media companies still use the theory today, although they often dispute, modify, and reconfigure the concept in an effort to fit new parameters. The original theory basically states that three is the magical number for frequency: the first exposure generally generates a "What is it?" response from the viewer. Although this is a great start, the theory further purports that a viewer generally discards anything new, thus requiring a second exposure. The viewer's response to the second exposure is, "How does this apply to me?" Clearly perceived as a progression process, the belief is that the viewer has already processed what it is and how it does or does not apply before the third exposure occurs, which serves as a reminder, therefore prompting action. According to Krugman, "There is a myth in the advertising world that viewers will forget a message if the message isn't repeated often enough. This idea supports most large advertising expenditures. I would rather say the public comes closer to forgetting nothing they have seen on TV. They just 'put it out of their minds' until and unless it has some use . . . and [then] the response to the commercial continues."

Unfortunately, the frequency theory is out of date. I recently cleared my living room end tables in front of the television and put away three tablets, a Game Boy, a laptop, and two smartphones, making it abundantly clear to me that participants have the tools to immediately look up something that interests them the first time they hear about it. This takes place in conjunction with television more often than not. It's time to question the relevance of reach and frequency relevance in today's cluttered and frequently-edited-by-the-viewer media world. Reach and frequency are still important variables today; they just may not be the only ones.

In 1960, print media accounted for almost one-third of all media consumption. By 1980, it had already slipped to one-sixth, even before social and mobile entered the landscape. A recent Pew Internet study found that media habits have evolved significantly even since 2000, describing today's habits as "pervasive, portable, personalized and participatory." Yet, another recent report on digital media found that Americans spend 1 hour and 21 minutes more time per day participating with media than they did in 2001. Not only is interaction time increasing, but so is the *amount of advertising*.

A recent Yankelovich study described how Americans are confronted by more than 5,000 selling messages per day. Ipsos OTX, a global market research company that specializes in advertising, loyalty, marketing, media, and public affairs market research, published a study in 2010 that reported that most people spend more than half their day interacting with media. Media saturation, the frequency factor, and even more specifically, the "three times media to action factor" are all important elements to consider when conducting a media buy today. The frequency formula was not created for the saturated media world we live in today, because it does not account for the participant's involvement in the purchase process: searching, researching, inviting friend input on social media sites, and spending time on sites where he or she learns what others have to say about the product or service. It also does not account for brands' ability to utilize data to inform media investment decisions.

Media agencies have long been the owners of the media formulas, and most brands expect their media partners to apply these formulas to achieve an appropriate marketing return. Although reach and frequency are still are still significant in the participatory world, they are by no means the *only* variables at play—and this is the distinction. Data management and integration become equally relevant. Insight from companies managing vast quantities of participant data indicates that any theory based on individual decisions may not apply when individuals are influenced by two other individuals during the decision-making process. Data are now revealing the complexity of persuasion and decision making, and this insight is likely to continue to transform future marketing models.

The initial media formulation and the actual media buy are only the beginning; in participation marketing, ongoing optimization becomes critical. It may be difficult for brands to authorize agencies to take into account the upfront media decisions and the entire campaign optimization, given the sensitive nature of certain data sets required for optimization, not to mention privacy considerations. It's equally challenging to segregate media by channel and not manage them holistically, as there is undoubtedly an overlap between channels that has an impact on effectiveness.

A number of companies are still using working versus nonworking media as a reference to the overall cost efficiency of marketing creation versus exposure. Before the Participation Age, this was a relatively reasonable way for brands to evaluate their marketing budget allocation. The notion originally came about in the 1980s, when media and creative agencies separated to develop distinct areas of expertise. Brands subsequently divided dollars between newly created and often independent functions of media and creative departments. As a result, companies created a rule of thumb for departmental budget planning and management. On average, they would invest 10 to 15 percent of their marketing budget for the marketing concept creation; another 15 to 20 percent on the actual production of the campaign; and the remaining 65 to 75 percent for media. In practice, the concept creation and production would be considered nonworking dollars, because they wouldn't see agency time in the creative development—or production of the campaign materials—until the actual campaign launch. Creative departments owned concept creation and production, that is, nonworking media. Media owned media, that is, working media.

Today, there is clearly a blurring of the lines in so many places, including between paid, owned, and earned media and technology, creative, and media. Even individual social platforms, such as Facebook and Twitter, are examples of how brands can leverage paid, earned, and owned media in a single environment. Brands such as Ford Motor Company are using advertisements (paid) to announce new vehicles and are driving traffic to their brand pages (owned), where they drive passion around specific brands, such as the Mustang, reaching fans who spread the word to their friends (earned). In the best and most effective campaigns, it is difficult to distinguish creative, media, and technology. Media is no longer considered an afterthought or just the execution; it can, and should, be considered a strategic element integrated into planning from the onset of the program. Most of our "revolutionary" clients evaluate all of their media as working. There is no room for waste in this highly competitive environment, and they are under pressure to squeeze the most out of every marketing dollar invested.

Share of Voice and Purchase Funnel

Another marketing tool that came about during the broadcast boom years is the idea of share of voice, something marketers measured to determine exactly how loud they were shouting compared with their competitors. The "loudness" of a competitor's shouting was generally equivalent to the amount dollars invested in the advertising medium.

I was responsible for working with various research firms to track Hewlett-Packard's share of voice and that of competitors for years. Toward the end of my tenure there, it clearly had become an exercise that revealed more about the depth of competitors' marketing pockets than anything else. At best, it was beneficial for providing insight to the timing of spend, and at times, it provided us a slight glimpse into competitive marketing spend strategy.

Share of voice is a classic push marketing tool that fails to capture today's earned or owned media. The closest relevant tool is perhaps social listening, which measures share of voices—in other words, the number of participants talking about you, what are they saying, and where are they saying it. Social listening asks: Are these conversations happening on properties you own or have influence over? How are you enabling the conversations that you believe are important to your business? Are you taking feedback from the conversation that you'll use to adapt your product and services and marketing plans? Are there industry trends or events that cause spikes in the voice about your brand? Are you taking advantage of leveraging these opportunities? These are all more valuable than simple share of voice measurement, which is why we'll cover this topic in more detail in the next chapter.

A technique called AIDA (attention, interest, desire, action) was developed before the turn of the twentieth century and was then correlated with share of voice calculations in the 1960s. As early as 1898, a man by the name of Elias St. Elmo Lewis mapped a theoretical customer journey from the moment a brand or product attracted consumer attention to the point of action or purchase:

Awareness: The customer is **aware** of the existence of a product or service.

Interest: The customer actively **expresses an interest** in a product group.

Desire: The customer **aspires to** own a particular brand or product.

Action: The customer **takes the next step toward purchasing** the chosen product.

This idea was applied to television in the 1960s. If a television commercial commanded enough attention (*awareness*), then that would drive a certain percentage amount of *interest* in the product or service being advertised. Of those interested, a certain percentage would have *desire*, and a subset of that group would eventually take *action*.

The purchase funnel is a similar linear concept. It's an illustration of the theoretical customer journey toward the purchase of a product or service, and it is one of the most prevalent models of the consumer's decision-making process used by marketers even today. Because of emphasis placed on measurement in our shift toward digital, this tool contributes to current conversations perhaps better than other, more outdated tools do. One of the funnel's additional benefits is that we can apply it to nearly every industry.

The purchase funnel is a close relative of AIDA in that it's a linear approach to communications theory. It assumed that in order for marketing to be effective, the consumer must undergo a sequence of mental events, with each stage dependent on the success of the previous stage, producing a funnel-like progression toward a purchase. The narrower the funnel, the closer the individual is to making the actual purchase.

Although developed half a century ago, linear sequential models such as the purchase funnel still provide the basic metaphor and language for marketers today. This is because the logic of the sequence seems scientifically irrefutable and comforting when seeking a simple approach to making an investment. There appears to be a direct correlation between investment and return—and the supposed stages actually do lend themselves readily to objective measurement. This is why brands still invest in television. They believe if they can invest $25 million into the top 10 markets on television in a week, they will see a corresponding and predictable percent lift in retail sales based on prior experience and measurement.

The challenge is that the funnel does not accurately *map* the participant's approach to a considered purchase decision in the participatory landscape. Let's take the automotive category, for example. Even in a dated 2004 New Autoshopper.com Study, approximately 50 percent all new-vehicle buyers indicated that their selection of the make and model and the price they paid or were offered were affected by information they found on the Internet—up from about 40 percent in 2002. Today's auto shoppers are even more aware of features and even inventory than most sales representatives. The purchase funnel does not consider how participants use online research to expand their consideration set, taking advantage of the experience of existing owners to help guide their choices. Both points have important implications for the purchase funnel.

A more recent study of online search behavior revealed that generic terms account for the majority of online search activity associated with a subsequent purchase. The study of search behavior in the electronics industry category indicated that generic product search terms (such as "camera," "HD television," or "smartphone") accounted for more than 70 percent of total search volume, whereas trademarked retailer terms (such as "Best Buy," "HP.com") accounted for 20 percent and specific product terms (such as "Canon digital camcorder," "HP elite book") accounted for only 10 percent. It also reported that although 85 percent of searchers conduct additional electronic category searches later in the shopping process, the majority of participants continue to use the same search term type (either generic or branded) with which they began the search process. We found this to be true at HP, especially related to the strength of branded terms.

Global digital business analytics firm comScore also found that generic search terms are likely to have influenced even those participants who did purchase after conducting a retailer trademark search (such as "Best Buy" or "HP"). Of these buyers, 84 searched using a

generic term earlier in the buying cycle, which emphasizes how crucial it is to reach participants early in the search process when they
are defining their consideration set. These data points challenge one
assumption that the purchase funnel makes: namely, that most participants begin the product search process by using a generic search
term (such as "HD TV") and then later refine their search activity to
product-specific terms (such as "Sony HD 4600"). At Performics, we
have found that nearly every searcher and every individual brand and
category have their own search journey, which makes it difficult to
broadly assume anything about searching patterns. There is not a predictable, linear path to purchase—as much as we would like it to be a
predictable path.

Let's go back to the automotive category. CNW Marketing
Research, a firm that sets the industry standard measurement of
automotive purchase behavior, has historically reported that buyers begin their purchase quest with six or seven vehicle models in
their consideration set, likely attributed to information and
recommendations for additional vehicles along their journey.
Then, over approximately six months, they refine the list
down to the one or two vehicles that they will test drive. Recent
annual tracking studies from CNW reveal that around halfway
through this process, the number of models investigated jumps
back *up* to around five or six models, revealing that new make
and model considerations are generated by online searches for
information. In other words, participants are actually discovering
cars that had not originally been in their consideration set when
using technology tools to research information. Manufacturer
or competitor advertising may or may not be influencing buyers in this process. Search has enabled participants to discover
a wealth of product and service information. In addition, posts
from influencers and current and past owners discussing their
ownership experiences certainly influence buyers.

It's also necessary to consider media clutter. The messaging clutter in 1898 or even 1960 was unquestionably different than it is today. The logic behind the purchasing funnel correlates relatively well to the share of voice broadcast model because it supports the idea that the more money an advertiser spends to achieve sufficient share of voice, the more it will ultimately drive action. The purchase funnel concept is used in marketing to guide promotional campaigns that target different stages of the customer journey. It can be used as a basis for customer relationship management (CRM) programs, as well as level of spend. However, the sheer quantity of information participants intercept in the cluttered world today suggests that it would take an enormous spend to result in action. It also assumes participants are not in control of the flow of that information.

Despite its shortcomings, I do not propose we throw the purchase funnel entirely out the window. What I *do* suggest is that rather than viewing it from the side as a wide mouth that becomes progressively narrower, we lower the funnel and peer into it from the top and view the items spinning around in a circular motion of a perpetual spiral. The goal is to keep the spiral spinning (see Figure 3.1).

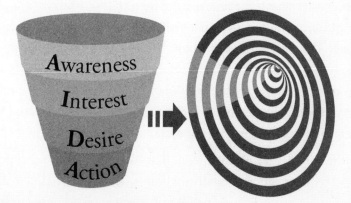

Figure 3.1 Participant Marketing Spiral

Until recently, we have not been able to create a scaled, intelligent, measurable model for media investments, even for purely digital buys. We can do it in pieces, but the fact that the model has not scaled well makes it difficult to connect the pieces to create the continuous loop. Marketers do not feel comfortable investing in programs that do not scale, especially given the recent resource belt-tightening resulting from the economic downturn. The reality is that the participant base has shifted and the digital medium is no longer young. It's time for the marketing industry as a whole to commit to the environment in which we are now living and invest in the infrastructure and resources that allow this to occur at scale. We will talk more about the marketing spiral in future chapters.

At HP, we used a number of models to describe our marketing plans and effectiveness. Another of the more common models is referred to at the four Ps. American marketing professor E. Jerome McCarthy proposed a four Ps classification in 1960, and the model was then commonly adopted by many marketers throughout the world. Obviously, the rise of technology and the dynamic, fragmented media environment have had a drastic effect on all four of the Ps as the landscape has changed dramatically since the model was created in the 1960s.

The first P stands for *product:* the item that satisfies what a consumer needs or wants and usually what the marketer is trying to promote. This portion is important, because each product or service experiences a life cycle comprised of an introduction, a growth phase followed by a maturity phase, and eventually, a period of decline. The idea was for marketers to devise different marketing tactics for different phases of the marketing cycle.

Although this hasn't changed today—marketers still must position and sell a product—the distinction is that the participant-driven market is now driving market demand. Participants provide product development input and are even building products themselves in some cases. Some companies today are creating products designed from the ground up by their customers. For example, consider a completely crowdsourced car like the Rally Fighter. Local Motors, the company behind the idea, invited participants to submit designs for the ideal car. They received 35,000 entries from nearly 3,000 community members in more than 100 countries. Since Local Motors does not employ designers, every component, interior and exterior, is off-the-shelf and open sourced. Even the name Rally Fighter was the result of a community vote. The end product is a $50,000 off-road (but street-legal) racing type of vehicle. The customers themselves complete the final assembly in local centers. Local Motors holds contests for the development, and the winner receives a monetary prize based on the importance of the system to developing the overall vehicle. This totally changes the intent of a manufacturing-driven product marketing approach.

The second P stands for *price:* the amount a customer pays for the product. This, of course, determines the company's profit. Decisions regarding the specific price affect the marketing strategy, the demand for the product, and sales. Price is considered an integral component to the other marketing Ps because it is critical to consider the customer-perceived value for the product.

But again, what happens in a marketplace where customers actually believe they can negotiate on price? And where powerful retailers, such as Amazon and Best Buy, offer discounts on products that drive overall demand—because of their powerful impact to the overall marketplace? Participants now understand that brands have to listen to them as they stand together to influence what once were decisions completely within manufacturer or retailer control. For example, Verizon decided in late 2011 to charge a $2 fee to customers who paid their wireless bills online. Customers reacted by protesting en masse and circulating an online petition—and Verizon retracted its decision just a day after it announced the fee. Around the same time,

Bank of America also decided against a new $5 monthly fee for debit card users after consumers called foul, which then drew the attention of lawmakers, who also protested the charge. Both companies recognized the power of their customers in their pricing decisions. They also understood that a prompt response and action was required. This situation is new for brands and would not have occurred 10 years ago.

The third P stands for *promotion*. This encompasses all methods of communication that a marketer may use to provide marketing communications about the product to different parties. It includes tactics such as advertising, public relations, personal selling, and sales promotion. Promotion was built on the premise that the marketer was in charge of all phases of push communications and focused on integrating the persuasive messages for the campaign. It was also built on the premise that awareness would build slowly through a controlled marketing approach, because communications was a barrier that faced all product demand. In the Participation Age, however, nearly all communications are now *pull* vehicles, which, of course, changes the very nature of promotion. Participants now can stand in the aisle of a retail store and compare promotional offers from multiple retailers, again giving them the power to influence the competitive transparency that surrounds promotion.

The final P stands for *place* and refers to the place or location convenient for consumers to purchase. This meant distribution and, from a marketing standpoint, often meant point-of-purchase communications, such as in-store merchandising. Obviously, there are many nuances to consider for placement in today's marketplace. Even the process of developing the cover designs for this book is an example. One of the primary considerations when I reviewed cover designs was how the book would appear online—on Amazon's site, for example— not just on the physical shelf in a store. Times have changed, and distribution and merchandising have a suite of new considerations that didn't come into play in the 1960s.

Above the Line

It's hard to comprehend how often the industry term *above the line* is used, given, in my experience, that most marketers do not know what it really means or where it originated. *Above the line* is most commonly used as a reference to mass-market advertising, generally branding campaigns, as opposed to direct mail, direct television (DRTV), and other transactional-based marketing activities.

Broadly speaking, the original reference is actually quite surprising. *Above the line* is not a marketing industry term at all, but rather one from the financial industry. The advertising reference came about during the early years of television, when creative agencies earned a commission by placing television advertisements, something they didn't get for newspaper ad placements. *Above the line* is an advertising accountancy term that referred to the creative that could be produced for free because the commission earned was lucrative. Print advertising did not earn agencies a commission. Can you imagine media companies earning enough commission today to pay for creative development? And this term truly doesn't make sense at all in our simultaneously highly fragmented and aggregated media environment. It is amusing that most marketers are not aware of where or how *above the line* came about, yet it still readily comes out of their mouth when discussing media or their marketing programs.

A great way to prompt people to pause is to simply ask, as I often do, where search or other digital channels sit: below the line or above the line? The answer, after a fair pause and puzzlement (because marketers know that television is always above the line but are not sure why this is the case), is usually "both." Given what we now know about the definition, the answer is "neither."

It is enlightening to look in the rearview mirror to determine how and why we got here. It's always surprising to me how many senior marketers so readily use the language of our business without truly comprehending its history or context. The revealing, crystallized moment for me—when I stopped to think, wait, and ask, "Why are we doing this?"—started me on that journey of understanding. Therefore, when I ask the question, I often get responses such as, "It's what I know" or "We have always done marketing this way." These answers are no longer adequate.

Many marketers argue that they are doing things differently because they are now managing Facebook programs instead of just buying television. Yet they're still relying on dated performance metrics inside Facebook, such as reach, in a medium where participation is just as important if not more so. comScore's 2012 study "The Power of Like 2" found that although the majority of large brands are active in social media marketing, the objective for these programs still is increasing the number of Facebook fans—in other words, managing reach. This is consistent with what we have found to be true working with clients at Performics. Brands like to measure Facebook fans as their primary marketing objective for the social space. They fail to ask themselves the larger subsequent questions: "What do we *do* with the fans now that we have them? What should engagement look like? How do I empower them to advocate for the brand and become a part of the marketing program? How do I enable amplification, thereby allowing these fans to connect with others who are also passionate about the brand and to connect with the brand itself? How do I, as a brand, become a Facebook participant myself?"

The Participation Age is a time of transition for marketers. We are all using the tools of our trade as we were taught—and we're being taught these tools because they were considered the most effective for their time. Looking back helps us to move forward, and understanding why the tools were developed lets us determine why and how we can evolve these tools for marketing in today's world. For those managing digital tactics, this often means having a conversation with marketing senior leaders because they need to be comfortable enough with change for the organization to endorse it and embrace it. These leaders have succeeded throughout their entire marketing careers by using tools developed for persuading customers in a reach-based marketing environment.

In fact, IBM recently interviewed more than 1,700 chief marketing officers (CMOs) from 64 countries around the globe. Their interviews revealed that the biggest challenges were the explosion of data, social media, the proliferation of channels and devices, and shifting consumer demographics. The study, which was titled "From Stretched to Strengthened: Insights from the Global Chief Marketing Officer," found that regardless of their company size or geographic location, CMOs overwhelmingly stated that their largest challenge as well as their biggest opportunity was to confront older mass-marketing assumptions, skill sets, and approaches. At a time when CMOs are doing more than they ever have before, the industry lacks new standardized tools and methods. As a result, CMOs revert back to what they know, and because there is no reliable alternative, they trust it. They don't have the time or energy to invent something. Of the CMOs interviewed, 79 percent believe the level of complexity will be high or very high over the next five years, yet only 48 percent feel prepared to cope with it. Even though they don't know how or why traditional tools and processes were created, they do understand a new path forward is vital.

In order to change, we must bridge what we know about our past and apply it to new models for the future. We must make an effort to embrace the newly empowered participants and foster lasting, reciprocal relationships with them, while at the same time measuring the results of our marketing in an effort to demonstrate value to our organizations.

Participant Marketing Summary

1. Hackers were instrumental in the rise of radio and television, which is not dissimilar to how the Internet first took root.

2. The digital revolution has many parallels to the broadcast revolution that occurred in the 1950s and 1960s.

3. Nearly all marketing tools, processes, and language were created in the broadcast era. The tools are linear and logical, and they are based on delivering a one-way persuasive message to broad groups of audiences.

Original Marketing Definitions

Above the line: An accountancy term that refers to the creative that could be produced for free given the substantial commission earned on the media placement for broadcast.

AIDA (awareness, interest, desire, action): A television commercial commanded enough attention to drive *awareness* that would then drive a percentage of *interest* to the product or service being advertised. Of those interested, a certain percentage would have *desire*, and a subset of that group would eventually take *action*.

Four Ps: Product, price, promotion, and placement.

Frequency: Based on the actions caused by the number of exposures to a message; the ideal number is thought to be three. The first exposure communicates what a product or service is. The second causes the audience to speculate how this product or service applies to the target. The third is a reminder to take some form of action.

Purchase funnel: An illustration of the theoretical customer journey toward the purchase of a product or service.

Reach: The total number of individuals or households exposed to an ad, at least once, during a given period of time. It can be stated as an absolute number or a fraction of a given population.

Working/nonworking media: The cost of the distribution of media is considered working, whereas creative development is nonworking.

Participant Marketing Questions

When planning marketing programs in the Participation Age, consider these questions:

1. Am I using old or new language?

2. How do I empower participants to activate my brand, product, or service?

3. How am I enabling amplification in my program planning?

4. How am I acting as a participant?

5. Am I a content creator and curator?

6. Am I enabling participants to connect with me and with other participants?

4 Time for a Participation Revolution

The advent of the first marketing textbooks containing the methods we know and use today, along with the tools, processes, and language, came about as a result of the large media disruptors of radio and then television. Yet all of the advertising-supported content models that were generated when broadcast media emerged are evaporating with the growth of the Internet. Marketing graduates entering the workforce to join agencies and brands, as well as marketing educators, know that these older tools aren't suitable; however, they struggle to find alternatives. A recent review of several widely used marketing texts produced a few mentions of the Internet and a paragraph or two on analytics and marketing measurement. It's clear that although mass media may survive, the rules participants, brands, and agencies follow when conducting marketing have all changed. It's time for a new participation and performance marketing model to take center stage.

Ironically, doing business in today's participation culture more closely resembles marketing 200 years ago. From the beginning of time, individuals have participated in the exchange of goods and services. Marketing has always been about relationships and communication among individuals negotiating a value exchange. The process is also about competency and understanding, even competitiveness and empowerment. We are, of course, still very much human, and our transaction behavior still reflects this, despite the technology that drives today's information and transactions. We still—and always will—need to have good information to make decisions, feel empowered that the decision is ours, and have trust within the negotiation.

Today's environment requires more sophisticated frameworks. Marketers need to learn to love data or, at the very least, embrace it. Historically, a number of marketing communications professionals ended up in the profession partly because they don't like math but are masters at words and ideas, but marketing is now about an elegant blend of art and science. Some of the most interesting marketing individuals I know began their career as mathematicians first and made the transition to marketing. Both art and science have a vital role in participation media. A new marketing solution must contain three variables to survive in the Participation Age:

1. **It should express our basic requirements as humans and be more biological and less mechanistic.** This is part of the transition from a more industrial age to the Participation Age. We are making decisions with our hearts now more than ever, and we are using technology and devices to supply logic and data to support those decisions.

2. **It must embrace the new data-enriched marketing approach.** This is something that will only increase as more sophisticated technologies are introduced—and as we continue to see growth in the number of devices that we use to exchange information and conduct transactions. The adoption of immediate information at our fingertips will continue to provide both participants and marketers with limitless information at all times.

3. **It must contain traces of traditional marketing methods.** It has to bridge the techniques that marketers have employed for past 50 or 60 years—because change is difficult, organizations are complex and have been constructed to support traditional models, and senior executives know, understand, and trust only traditional methods and are rewarded for traditional metrics.

These are all reasons why we can't expect to adapt to a new model overnight.

The complex challenges of the new media landscape are simultaneously precipitating a change and complicating the solution. There are two seemingly contradictory trends currently under way. On one hand, new media technologies have lowered production and distribution costs in the media industry itself. This has, in turn, expanded the range of available delivery channels and enabled participants to archive, annotate, appropriate, and redistribute media content in powerful new ways.

The Internet now enables media that works both for group-distributed information as well as individual conversations. This has never happened in the history of media. When I was 14, I couldn't wait to spend an hour on the telephone talking to my best friend after school. Because she lived 5 miles away, this was the only way I could have a one-to-one conversation with her. And if I wanted to have a conversation with more than one of my friends at a time, we, of course, had to gather at the same place at the same time, which always took effort and time to coordinate. Consider the multitude of choices my children have today for having one-to-one and one-to-many conversations: text, chat, e-mail, Facebook, Twitter, Pinterest . . . the list goes on. It takes virtually no time for them to connect with a friend individually or to converse with a group of friends. And people's expectations of time have changed along with the changing media landscape and technology adoption. It used to be very difficult to have a one-to-one conversation with a customer and there were very few choices for one-to-many message distribution. There was also no way for the many to respond.

Media now occurs at the same time events do. This is also a new phenomenon—and has come about as a result of the social element of technology. Despite the fact that ownership of mainstream commercial media has become increasingly consolidated, control over media in general is slipping. There are numerous examples of newsworthy stories being first reported not by an authorized media source but via an individual's Twitter post. An environment that is increasingly social, global, local, and unstandardized has replaced the old reach-based controlled and homogeneous media landscape.

Even the Internet continues to change as more devices and the diversity of those devices access it. Internet marketing has progressively developed since 1995, based on the notion that everything is connected and the Internet works because it has a set of universal standards. Now, each new device—be it an iPad, phone, Android, or Kindle—has its own individual ad network, format, and technology. Each new social site has an individual log-in, and many of these sites hide content from search engines. Each often has its own complex network. Some are referring to this as the splinternet, implying this can cause an overabundance of new headaches for marketers trying to apply the old reach approach to media standardization. The new environment is anything but standardized.

Dated philosophies dominate our marketing industry. Even education institutions and curricula have been late to catch up; there are few alternatives to address the complexity of the environment and break through the stalwart traditions of the familiar processes and methods. Education and brand marketing departments alike are just now beginning to consider alternatives, but we need *radical* change—and we need it now. The fortune hidden in the recent economic downturn is that it has caused a transformation in our industry to occur faster, for both participants and marketers.

So, how do we begin a participant marketing revolution today and take the first step to reinvent our old marketing methods? We start by embracing the ingredients of a new marketing method called the *Participation Way* as a way to begin seeding participant marketing into our traditional organizations, which requires that we break the habits of an industry that has been more than 60 years in the making. We can start overcoming this challenge by more carefully choosing the words we use every day and then using these new terms to incorporate a planning process with fresh tools and philosophies.

For 60 years, marketers have focused on broadcasting a message via the reach and frequency model. The decades-old process of designing a marketing program for potential customers to "consume a message" is over. Action programs are required for action mediums, as well as for immediacy and continuous programs. Participants expect to have an ongoing relationship with brands. The always-on factor, by itself, is a significant expectation shift for marketers. Traditional marketing tools and processes are designed for a launch followed by "wait and see." But today's immediate and constant access to a device with limitless information means program integration is absolutely crucial; marketers must plan every touch point and every moment in advance and be prepared for a program that is enduring.

The notion of participant marketing was bit before its time when I first began thinking about starting a marketing revolution in 2005. It was certainly premature compared with today's headlines, in which participants have fully recognized the shift and are taking a stand to occupy Wall Street and are using technology to motivate others to take part in a cause to overthrow governments. Taking on a brand seems easy by comparison.

During the past few years, access to technology and information has literally changed expectations. The new participants have expectations of a reciprocal relationship and empowerment. They have evolved and have begun to have expectations of having a dialogue, an interaction. Having a campaign that worked well and invited participation has become much more important than simply having a big idea or stunningly beautiful creative that someone watched but didn't touch. In the past, our job involved creating something that was persuasive and that would change perception; we now have to *motivate participation*. If it seems like an overwhelming task, this is likely not an overstatement. On a more positive note, this is a much more powerful and meaningful role for marketers; by creating a program designed to empower participation, we can begin to understand what motivates people in general, which affects much more than just marketing in an organization. It's more substantial and less "fluffy," as marketing has sometimes been labeled in the past.

Companies that develop platforms designed specifically for participation are poised for future growth. The countless Gen Yers who use Facebook every day are born as or evolved into participants who expect to engage with individuals and brands in an ongoing relationship, and they have mastered the tools that make it possible. Participation is innate to their identity—in the real world and in the virtual world. And the line separating these two worlds is becoming very thin. Companies are now challenged to hire these participants as employees *and* win them over as customers in the hopes of fostering lasting relationships. In both cases, it's absolutely crucial to create an environment designed for participation.

Despite thousands of years of writings about self-motivation and participation, none of this has been applied to the world of marketing. This is because marketing didn't lend itself to participation. But what if, as a brand, you were able to employ motivational theory to your marketing programs? The Participation Way is designed to provide three simple ingredients to your marketing programs modeled after the three primary principles of the self-determination theory of competence, autonomy, and relatedness. These ingredients are based on human behavior that psychologists and sociologists have studied for decades regarding what motivates people to take part in something. Participation science has never been something that mattered to marketers—before now. To harness it, we must first understand participation.

What is participation, exactly? *Participate* means "to take part, have a share and become something larger." What motivates people to do so has fascinated sociologists for a very long time. The concepts of self-determination theory and intrinsic motivation are more recent outcomes of these studies. Motivation theories are built on two sets of assumptions about how individuals have the incentive to take action. The mechanistic theory views the human organism as passive and led by the surrounding environment, whereas the organismic theory states that the human initiates the behavior and controls the environment—and is not passive at all.

Self-determination theory is based on the latter organismic theory or a more biological approach and assumes that humans' basic needs prompt psychological drives that provides energy for them to act *on*—rather than simply react *to*—the environment. These natural developmental tendencies do not, however, operate automatically; instead, they require ongoing social reinforcement. Social situations and environmental conditions can either support or hinder the natural tendencies toward active engagement and psychological growth. The study of self-determination theory discusses how environments and social context can be studied to nurture motivation and active engagement.

Self-determination theory, once referred to as drive theory, is an area of psychology that began with Sigmund Freud in 1914 and continued with C. L. Hull, who wrote *Principles of Behavior: An Introduction to Behavior Theory* in 1943. In his 1959 *Psychological Review* article titled "The Concept of Competence," R. W. White proposed the notion that organisms are innately motivated to be effective within their environment. These early theories about motivational force were often referred to as independent ego energy.

The scientific community has coalesced more recently around the idea that intrinsic motivation is based in our needs to be competent and self-determining. As mentioned previously, Richard M. Ryan and Edward L. Deci of the University of Rochester are more recent renowned experts in the field of self-determination theory. Their studies focus around three main criteria for environmental and social context for individuals to feel motivated to take part: the basic psychological needs for *autonomy, competence*, and *relatedness*.

The self-determination theory maintains that if a person's needs are continually satisfied, he or she will develop and function effectively and experience wellness. However, if one or all of these needs are not met, then he or she is less likely to thrive and experience optimal functioning.

Because the study is based on the contextual situations and associated environments, it has been applied to many fields where situations and environmental consideration are top of mind, such as education, organizational health and human resources, sports and physical activity, religion, health and medicine, parenting, virtual environments, close relationships, and psychotherapy. Marketers can draw an interesting correlation between the passive mechanistic theory, which drove marketing's former role of governing uninformed consumers, and the organismic theory, which drives today's approach of actively engaging informed participants. In a passive mechanistic view, marketers could provide a specific message that would then cause the appropriate response. But today's participatory environment requires the appropriate marketers to consider the social context and environmental conditions to instigate and perpetuate competence, autonomy, and relatedness.

These three principles are the cornerstone of the self-determination theory and have been slightly modified to form the Participation Way formula (Discover + Empower + Connect = Participation), which was developed as a guide for marketers seeking to inspire and motivate participation with a brand. It's important to understand all three from a sociological and psychological viewpoint, because they are critical to creating optimal conditions for participation and engagement. They are also intrinsically linked to provide an environment conducive to participation requires using all three components. It's also helpful to understand each individually, because the specific components are critical to the new participation planning tools discussed later in this book.

Achieving a Goal with Competence: In the Palm of Every Hand

It is somewhat unfortunate that I find myself in airports often—at least twice a week and sometimes more. One of my favorite pastimes is wandering through airport lounges, sneaking a glance over shoulders to see how people are occupying their time. The dedicated road warrior employee is what you'd expect, and surely there are plenty busily working their way through inboxes, creating presentations, or holding annoyingly loud conversations on their mobile phones to the chagrin of everyone sitting nearby.

The Red Carpet Club in the Chicago O'Hare airport attracts an odd combination of business travelers desperately seeking a quiet room, a soft seat, readily convenient electrical outlets, and a reliable Wi-Fi connection and weary travelers and their families who are trying their best *not* to work on their way to "getting away from it all."

More interesting are those intently focused on their iPhone or iPad screens. The calculated finger swipe is the simple give away: the pointer finger swipes to the left, followed by a fingertip lift and a pause of great anticipation; then another pause before the user repeats. Every once in a while this might be accompanied by a little satisfied smirk or aggravated purse of the lips. Sometimes, if you're lucky, you will even hear the annoying jingle that accompanies the familiar hand motions. I have counted more than 30 participants in a single airport lounge simultaneously engaged in the same puzzling task: they are all playing Angry Birds.

Created by a small game designer from Finland named Jaakko Iisalo, Angry Birds began when Iisalo was searching for an iPhone application in an effort to earn some extra dollars for Rovio, the small game development company where he worked. Since the game's creation in 2009, Angry Birds programs and applications have been downloaded more than a billion times. It has become the most popular and frequently installed out of the 300,000 available applications, and it has quickly spread to Apple's iPad as well. A later variation launch, Angry Birds Space, saw 10 million downloads in the first three days of its release. Twentieth Century Fox has made the popular game into a movie, likely spawning another swarm of downloads, and the company has earned untold revenue generated from apparel, mugs, plush animals, and ringtones. I would say Iisalo has accomplished his goal, given the fact that Angry Birds cost a mere $140,000 to create and has generated more than $100 million in revenue. Who would have thought that a gaggle of fat, round birds with prominent yellow beaks catapulted through the air toward a castle or some other stone or stick contraption would catch on as a major pastime on every device used today?

Yet Angry Birds is just one example of the kind of behavior that participative environments across a multitude of devices can inspire in the general population.

Mobile adoption, in particular, is perhaps the answer for companies that question the need to become more participant-focused. A mobile device is the ultimate tool for participants: it's a simple technology vehicle that provides competence and autonomy in the palm of one's hand. A majority of mobile phone users report that they consider the device to be so personal that they do not allow it to stray more than a foot away from their person 24 hours a day, seven days a week. The speed at which the mobile device has proliferated globally demonstrates its ability to activate participation, particularly with Gen Yers, who have adopted it at a phenomenal rate and use it in ways we digital immigrants never imagined.

It took 20 years for the first billion mobile phones to sell worldwide; the second billion sold in 4 years, and the third billion, in 2. It is now estimated that more than 5 billion people—about 62 percent of the planet's population—use mobile phones, compared with less than 2 billion who have a personal computer. A number of research firms indicate that this number is expected to reach 20 billion by the year 2020. Some say that the number of connected devices will surpass 50 billion by 2020. People on every continent are embracing mobile as the primary method for electronic communications. They use their phones for activities no one could have imagined even five years ago—from purchasing products and services to testing blood insulin levels to tracking the location of their pets. Advances in mobile networks, platforms, devices, and data have combined to create an extremely personal and participation-enabling device. Within just a few years, more people will be able to access the Internet from a mobile device than from any other technology.

The mobile phone has become a tool that feeds the human desire for competency and autonomy in developing nations—powerful enough to change economic and political landscapes. In areas such as Africa, Vietnam, and Afghanistan, participants are buying generators for the first time, not to cook a warm meal or bring electricity to light their homes, but to charge their mobile phones. Although portable generators have been available for decades, the demand is recent, and this new demand is exclusively tied to mobile phone use because phones need to be charged every two days. Without a generator, these individuals often needed to walk 2 hours or more each way to charge their devices. Smartphones have reached nearly a saturation point in China, where the government has begun transforming obsolete phone booths into Wi-Fi hot spots. The mobile phone infrastructure and device have helped change nearly every aspect of our lives: the manner in which we work, shop, interact with media, and most important, communicate.

From the time of birth, all living beings—including humans—require stimulation to function effectively. Humans have an innate curiosity and desire to continually learn. They also experience inherent satisfaction in exercising and extending their capabilities to impact someone or something else. According to Deci and Ryan, *competence* is the "accumulated result of one's interactions with the environment—including exploration, learning, and adaptation." The reward for competency-motivated behavior is the associated feeling that comes as a result of feeling capable about what we are doing. This is why someone feels better after accomplishing something that has been difficult to achieve.

The interesting part of this theory is that these feelings seem to result only when one is able to continually stretch his or her capabilities. Merely repeating the same tasks does not have the same positive effect. The topic of gaming is one area that many sociologists and psychologists have explored extensively, given its relevance to mastering levels of competence.

Autonomy and the Pyramids

The only remaining of the original seven wonders of the world and the oldest structure in existence, the Great Pyramid of Giza is arguably the most challenging structure ever to be built—even if construction were to be attempted today. Its mortar joints are consistently 1/50 inch, which is incredible craftsmanship considering that no stone in the more than 2 million stones that make up the pyramid weighs less than 1 ton. Most weigh approximately 2.5 tons, and some, as much as 20! This amazing structure is 30 times larger than the Empire State Building. Its base covers over more than 13 acres (equal to seven Midtown Manhattan city blocks), each side being greater than 5 acres in area.

It was believed until recently that slaves captured during the conquering of nearby countries built the pyramids. According to legend, these individuals were forced to travel to Egypt, where they unwillingly spent years constructing the pyramids at the direction of a merciless pharaoh. Hollywood has helped plant this image firmly into our minds. However, Egyptologists have made several recent discoveries that cast major doubts upon this theory. There are a few experts who now believe the pyramids may have been built by a combination of skilled workers and ordinary citizens who wanted to take part in a monumental challenge to help out their pharaoh. Some of the evidence is in the form of graffiti indicating that these workers took pride in their work, calling their teams Friends of Khufu and Drunkards of Menkaure, names indicating allegiances to pharaohs and an allegiance to one another.

This evidence is causing a lively debate among a number of archaeologists. Some believe the builders were slaves; others think they were participants. And still others believe the amazing architectural feats were mastered by a combination of the two. In any case, constructing a pyramid took an estimated 20 years, and regardless of who actually built one or what the hierarchical approach was, it's evident that the Egyptian people's success in building the awe-inspiring pyramids and mastering those skills has not affected their desire to continue to accomplish great things, especially in today's Participation Age when they are armed with technology.

Perhaps one of the most notable recent examples of social movement participation is the Arab Spring that took place in the Middle East. It began with the movement in Egypt, where people took on an incredible challenge: the nation's administration, notably, President Hosni Mubarak. It all began with an anti-Mubarak Facebook page created by Google's Middle East marketing manager, Wael Ghonim. Despite the fact he worked for Google, Ghonim was not a social media expert, nor was he an expert at Egyptian politics. He was simply someone who wanted to do something for a country he cared about—and he realized that he had the power to make a difference by using the technology of our socially connected environment.

The Facebook page Ghonim created encouraged millions of Egyptians to take part in a social movement demanding that

Mubarak step down after three decades of authoritarian rule. Even when the government made the unprecedented move to disconnect the country's Internet from the outside world for several days, Twitter and Google engineers developed a "Speak-to-Tweet" service that gave Egyptians a way to post to Twitter via voice messages sent from their mobile phones. Mubarak even sanctioned this "participant power"—perhaps unintentionally—by using it himself. He did not announce he was stepping down on CNN or the local news; he made the announcement on Facebook!

Before Egypt cut off the Internet and mobile phones—or even began blocking Twitter and Facebook—citizens used these tools to coordinate and spread the word about scheduled demonstrations. Without these forums, fewer participants would have known about the protests or summoned the kind of courage that made the uprising possible by knowing that others were willing to participate in the challenge. These tools of technology allowed them to feel as though they are making a difference with their own voices and inspired by the challenge at hand. It was a perfect storm for participation in today's connected world.

The Egyptian uprising demonstrates a new form of revolutionary politics defined not so much by the mass street protests but the way in which participants come together to resist control and determine the fate of their country. It's also another good example of how media has evolved into an underlying foundation of mass distribution and, simultaneously, socially fuelled conversations. This is a critical consideration for brands; they are dealing with participants who want to be informed and feel as though they are in control of their own decisions about a product or service. A recent research study titled "S-Net: A Study in Social Media Usage and Behavior"—commissioned by Performics and conducted by ROI Research—found that 56 percent of individuals believe that they can influence companies by voicing an opinion. Nearly 30 percent want to receive communications from brands about products and services more than once a week. A stunning 45 percent actually say that social network communications from companies and brands are replacing other communications channels for their source of information. Other participant groups indexed even higher, further illustrating how important autonomy and empowerment are to these individuals and how their expectations have shifted in today's environment.

Autonomy is a powerful self-determination principle, and it reinforces the desire for competency. This generally refers to a basic human need to control our environment or outcomes. In other words, it's less about control for the sake of the outcome and all about the control for the experience of freedom. Several studies determined that people do not always *want* control over their outcomes; they want a choice about *whether to be* in control. People need to feel free from dependence on outcomes over which they have control and, in fact, sometimes prefer *not* to control outcomes. Autonomy is a powerfully emotional ingredient of self-determination theory because it has the ability to enhance intrinsic motivation and provide a sense of competence. A number of studies have indicated that the need to *have a choice* matters more than *the outcome of the choice itself*, and there are numerous examples of this in the Participation Age.

Brands, companies, and countries are all just beginning to understand that this affects *how* they engage with their customers or constituents. A recent and well-known example is the Go Obama site. Although the president initially used this to gather participants to win the election, he has continued his dialogue with them throughout his presidency. Even in conversations in which President Obama has a differing opinion from even the most vocal and coalescing participants, he continues to allow them freedom of speech within the community—versus choosing to exert control and censor or delete conversations about specific topics.

Relatedness: The Social Network Explosion Connects People

A central California resident named Imogene has always enjoyed relationships. Her Facebook profile photo resembles a 1920s movie star. Just like the site's other 900 million users, Imogene logs on, responds to friend requests, and comments on pictures. But unlike most other Facebook participants, Imogene is 82 years old. She uses Facebook to share pictures of herself and her family on her page. It might be surprising that a grandmother uses her Facebook page in this way, but Imogene is not alone, but rather one of a growing number of Facebook participants older than age 50. Facebook is a comforting way to be surrounded by others by providing a great sense of acceptance and security for individuals of any age. It can also be a way for older individuals to connect with friends who may not be as mobile as they once were but who still crave community interaction.

Humans have an innate desire to interact; they operate best in an environment that provides a sense of acceptance and security. Facebook is a popular example of an environment designed for connecting participants. Although social networks often use all three ingredients of self-determination theory, we will focus on relatedness for this example. Can you think of a better way to continually connect with the people you care about? The Facebook environment provides visible, instantaneous acceptance and security in the form of status updates, photos, and celebration of significant events—multiple times every day.

Because of my busy travel schedule and weekly commute between at least two states, I had some trouble following the events taking place in my small community. Our weekly newspaper simply didn't quench my thirst for immediate local information, since most of it was outdated by the time I got around to reading it. I had stopped trying to keep up—that is, until I noticed a Facebook page for the county where I live. Because my college-aged son had "liked" the page, it showed up in my News Feed, and I suddenly found myself once again connected to my community. I discovered that the Farmer's Market starts on Friday, flu shots are available at the hospital or pharmacy, and there was a registration for an upcoming marathon due Friday—even daily notices about lost or found dogs were suddenly at my fingertips. One evening, the post was for a lost grandmother with dementia who had wandered away from a church. Amazingly, the Facebook community quickly connected and found her within 40 minutes!

My husband, who doesn't travel—and should theoretically know more about local happenings—asked me, "How to you know these things?" He "liked" the Facebook page and is now better informed too. The number of people following the page nearly equals the town's population. Because I originally saw this via my 20-something son, I assumed its author was a former high school classmate. But my assumption was incorrect. The woman in her 50s who curates the page receives most of her content from participants. She's a volunteer who takes satisfaction in creating and distributing content. Through her inspiration, the local newspaper and county government entities, such as the sheriff's department, have also created pages and link to her so she can curate and share content.

I am sure that many people besides me find the page far more useful than a subscription to the local newspaper. The page's author also has a personal Facebook page that she uses to connect with friends and promote her personal opinions. She uses the county page to disseminate less biased content and connect individuals to one another, and she continually invites participation by promoting photo contests and reposting content. She never thought her county page would displace the local weekly newspaper—and ironically, it hasn't. In fact, the local newspaper actually benefits by linking to her page and vice versa. This is a wonderful example of how the media-controlled, document-driven web has evolved to a participant-driven web.

According to Facebook's self-reported statistics, at the time this was written, Facebook had more than 900 million active users globally—approximately one Facebook member for roughly every nine people on the planet. The site has more than 70 translations available, and more than 80 percent of its users are located outside the United States. Facebook penetration rates for countries outside the United States are extremely high. For example, 90 percent of Internet users in Singapore participate on Facebook. In Italy, this number is 60 percent, and in Canada, 63 percent. Facebook is the second most visited site in the United States, with a penetration rate of 63 percent, behind Google and ahead of YouTube and Yahoo! Fifty percent of active users log on every day and spend more than 700 billion minutes per month participating. Two hundred fifty million users primarily access Facebook via mobile devices, and those who do are spending *twice* as much time there as those who access the site via other means.

Every 60 seconds, Facebook users send more than 230,000 messages, update 95,000 statuses, write 80,000 wall posts, tag 65,000 photos, share 50,000 links, and contribute 500,000 comments. Each participant has an average of 130 friends. There are more than 900 million objects with which participants interact: pages, groups, events, and community pages, to name a few. The average participant interacts with 80 community pages, groups, and events. Participants create 90 pieces of content each month and share more than 30 billion pieces of this content, which includes web links, news stories, blog posts, notes, and photo albums. And they install 20 million applications every day.

Participants have also helped to *develop* Facebook. More than 300,000 users helped translate the site through the translations application, and developers from more than 190 countries build applications and programs using Facebook Platform.

Brands operate within Facebook as equal participants. Those with the most fans at the time of publication are Coca-Cola, with 22 million; Starbucks, with 19 million; Oreo, with 16 million; Disney, with 16 million; and Red Bull, with 15 million. Let's look closer at the first two on this list. Although Starbucks' website attracts nearly 2 million visitors monthly and Coca-Cola has 270,000 visitors monthly, their Facebook pages get nearly 20 million and more than 22 million, respectively. This is roughly 10 times the traffic on their company websites. Coca-Cola has developed a highly coordinated global strategy that taps the strategies of the Participation Way by using their 25-million-strong fan base to create space for "local" content within a single fan page. The brand achieves big participation numbers by providing a rich diversity of choice and local directions within their Facebook page.

Retailers such as Walmart and Target aggressively use Facebook to evaluate new products. Cabela's, a hunting, fishing, camping, and outdoor gear retailer, engages nearly 2 million passionate fans about everything from game recipes to trivia; it also allows fans to showcase their hunting and fishing achievements. Facebook is quickly adapting and providing tools that enable brands to gain valuable insight. For example, Facebook can help all brands measure the second level of impact of brand fan pages—meaning what happens beyond the "like."

The participant-driven Internet is driving an increasingly interconnected world. Every month, more than 250 million people engage with Facebook on external websites. Since the company launched social plug-ins in April 2010, more than 2.5 million websites have integrated with Facebook, an average of 10,000 new websites every day. These include more than 80 of comScore's US Top 100 websites and over half of comScore's Global Top 100 websites. These include sites such as Yahoo!, AOL, CBS, Amazon, *New York Times*, and others. The share plug-in has provided obvious value for Facebook, but what they are contributing to other sites is even more telling.

For example, within a number of months following Facebook integration to its website, the *Washington Post*'s site traffic increased by 280 percent.

And, as the Imogene example clearly demonstrated, Gen Yers are not the only ones caught up in the new social network craze. In fact, the largest-growing segment on Facebook is the older-than-30 age group. *All* individuals, of all ages, desire to connect with others, and social platforms foster an environment rich with opportunity. Brands must remember they are participants too, and therefore, they have a responsibility to relate in a manner consistent with communal environments. They must keep in mind that they are active participants who look out for others' well-being, with responsibility, cooperation, compassion, and respect. Brands often help facilitate communities for the purpose of connecting to the brand, but this is also about facilitating community among participants.

Relatedness is about the need to feel connected to others— humans' intrinsic desire to belong and be part of something. Technology helps facilitate relatedness by allowing individuals anywhere in the world with like minds and interests to connect at any time of day—prompting them to feel as though they belong to a larger community.

In a broader sociological construct, relatedness helps moderate autonomy, encourage symmetry, and balance our first-person view of the world, and it allows us to interact effectively with others. We can give and accept responsibility, cooperation, compassion, and respect. Community encourages relatedness, and relatedness encourages community. An essential concept in combining autonomy with relatedness is recognizing where one person's rights and responsibilities end and another's begin. The autonomous person understands the extent and importance of this and bases mature decisions on this understanding. These are all important foundational elements of self-determination theory: competence, autonomy, and relatedness. Now, we can move to the more actionable and simplified version of self-determination theory designed specifically for marketing application: the Participation Way.

Participant Marketing Summary

1. Marketing has always been about relationships and communication among individuals negotiating a value exchange. It's also about competency, understanding, and empowerment. In essence, we are still very much human, which our transaction behavior reflects—despite the technology that drives information and even transactions today. We still need to have good information to make informed decisions; we need to feel empowered that the decision is ours, and we need to have trust within the negotiation.

2. A new marketing solution must contain three variables to survive in the Participation Age:

   a. It should express our basic requirements as humans and be more biological and less mechanistic.

   b. It must embrace the new data-enriched marketing approach.

   c. It must contain traces of traditional marketing methods and bridge the traditional marketing techniques employed for past 50 or 60 years.

3. The Internet now enables media that works both for group-distributed information and for individual conversations. This has never happened in the history of media.

4. In the past, marketers' jobs involved creating something persuasive that would change perception. Now, our job is to *motivate participation*. The participatory environment requires marketers to consider the social context and environmental conditions to instigate and perpetuate competence, autonomy, and relatedness.

5. Competence, autonomy, and relatedness are the cornerstones to the Participation Way formula, which was developed as a guide for marketers seeking to inspire and motivate participation with a brand. It's important to understand all three from a sociological and psychological viewpoint; they are critical to creating optimal conditions for participation and engagement. They are also intrinsically linked; providing an environment conducive to participation requires using all three components.

5 Participation Way for the Participation Age

There were a number of examples cited earlier regarding how the elements of competence, autonomy, and relatedness are relevant in today's Participation Age. Obviously, although these examples illustrated individual ingredients, all the ingredients are connected. They are not independently discrete. This is important, because a number of marketers still wonder whether it's sufficient to incorporate just one or two elements. We know now that this is not possible. Each principle is both individual in what it represents and highly connected with the others. Furthermore, today's connected world weaves these relationships together even more closely. As mentioned in the previous chapter, Facebook is a great example of an environment that embraces and uses all three principles very effectively.

For example, we know that mobile devices enable participants to find new information and become more competent. In addition, there are more than 250 million active users currently accessing Facebook through their mobile devices. As cited in the previous chapter, Facebook participants who use mobile devices are two times more active than users who access the site via other means. We live in a connected world that, each year, sends more than 11 trillion e-mails and more than 6 trillion text messages, posts tens of billions of tweets and Facebook status updates, "checks in," and more.

Tim O'Reilly's concept of Web 2.0 was first promoted at a 2004 conference of key industry leaders. It later spread via the "What Is Web 2.0?" essay that he coauthored with John Battelle (author, founder, and chairman of Federated Media Publishing, *Wired* magazine, and the *Industry Standard*). The original Web 2.0 essay encoded the "best practices" of companies—Amazon, Yahoo!, and Google, among them—that had survived the dot-com meltdown and offered advice for those who wanted to capitalize on the opportunity that this new reality offered. The essay describes a world where companies are able to "harness the collective intelligence" and circulate "user-generated content"; where the key component of any new opportunity requires developing what O'Reilly called "architecture of participation"; and where participant-led innovation fuels the ongoing innovation, technologies, and even marketing methods. The Participation Way is intended to be a tool for this new generation of marketing tools and for the "architecture of participation."

The Participation Way came about five years ago, shortly after I left Hewlett-Packard (HP). As described in Chapter 1, I had concluded that there was a new need for tools and processes, and I even had coined the phrase *participant marketing*. This insight prompted my move to the marketing agency Moxie Interactive, where I pioneered some relevant new tools designed specifically for participation planning, tools that used social listening, along with briefing tools for campaign planning that were more about action than communication or perception. There was no longer a question in my mind that marketing programs specifically designed to inspire participation were more effective. The missing ingredient was the *science* behind participation motivation. However, I am a marketer, not a scientist—and I understood the importance of having the new tools and philosophies built on sociological and psychological principles. Marketing tools have always been built on these principles. Emotional benefit laddering, first introduced by Thomas J. Reynolds and Jonathan Gutman in 1988 and based on Gutman's means-end theory of 1982, has been used for decades to determine the right message to communicate about a product or service. But this process was about changing perceptions, not inciting action.

After about two years of research, I decided to focus on the previously described theories of intrinsic motivation and self-determination. I did a great deal of research and eventually created a framework specifically designed for marketing purposes. The idea was to apply self-determination principles to marketing programs and thereby fundamentally change the philosophy, in addition to the planning tools, to effect behavior change. I also began to talk about the Participation Way—even though in those days we had not yet named it as such. And in doing so, I discovered how compelling the idea of participant marketing was to both marketing and agency professionals, something that remains true today. Most brands are faced with significant and compelling marketing pain points, and everyone is struggling with the same problem: the old tools simply do not work in the new environment.

The three major goals for the Participation Way framework follow:

1. **Simple:** The framework should be in an easy-to-understand and easy-to-remember format. I'm a big fan of developing frameworks that consist of no more than three of anything. We are all busy people; complicated frameworks are great if one has the time and energy to make them work. But most of us don't. Agencies and client organizations have become very lean; they frequently face talent turnover and need to train year-round. Digital talent, in particular, is scarce. Nearly all organizations have experienced downsizing to their organizations, with turnover being especially high in digital marketing. A number of research sources indicate that most companies still have fewer than 10 individuals in the entire organization managing digital disciplines—and talent acquisition and retention are key issues for them. Therefore, a simple approach that is easy to remember, explain, and transfer is crucial. A marketer's world is complicated enough; there is no use for intricate methods or theories.

2. **Grounded in science:** Many agencies and consultants use frameworks with logical merit based on engagement, content, or social

amplification. However, many of these lack specificity for why or how social amplification occurs. Nearly everyone understands the importance of considering content and social elements; what we *really* need is a formula for creating marketing programs that work well in today's environment. Content and engagement are good thought starters, and they certainly are better than no discussion about amplification or social discovery. However, they are not enough. Incredibly, there are still plenty of communications planning briefs that focus solely on one-way transmission of information or creative big ideas. I have not seen any frameworks based on sociological or psychological motivational theory and how to inspire participation. The goal is to create a framework and associated planning tools to support participation inspiration.

3. **Actionable:** Frameworks are great in theory, but they are valuable only if a marketer can actually *use them* to create meaningful programs. And because our world today is so focused on performance and data, we must also develop a model that allows us to measure early in the process. Long gone are the days when we developed a marketing communication strategy and the associated campaign and then took a break before examining the program more thoroughly several months later to see if it was effective. Today, the work originates several months before the launch date, starting with planning; then the real work begins at launch itself. We now have the measurement tools and processes that enable us to constantly adjust our marketing tactics to drive efficiency and effectiveness, taking advantage of active trends in the marketplace that may or may not be driven by our own program. And we have the ability to respond and adjust to participant actions. A good framework needs to take this into account and aid the marketer all along the way.

These parameters, along with the principles of intrinsic motivation and self-determination theory, are the basis for the Participation Way.

Table 5.1 describes how the Participation Way framework correlates with self-determination theory principles—specifically, the attributes of competence, autonomy, and relatedness.

Although adapted from intrinsic motivation and self-determination theory, the Participation Way framework is designed specifically for marketers. Although the self-determination principles are nouns that describe a state of the environment, it is important for the Participation Way elements to be verbs. This is because the goal of marketing in the Participation Age is to invite, encourage, and nurture participation; therefore, the marketing framework should be grounded in a plan that focuses on motivating participants to *take action*.

The first time I experienced the potential success that could be achieved using the Participation Way framework was in the fall of 2007. I was working on the "What do you have to say?" printing campaign for HP, and we developed a number of very early programs designed for the participant marketing landscape. This was quite unintentional, as we didn't really understand consciously that we were doing it at the time. However, it was one of the earliest instances where I began understanding that creating effective integrated marketing programs in this new landscape required us to think differently about marketing.

This was before I understood incentive drivers or intrinsic motivation, but it instigated my search for a scientific basis and new planning tools, which occurred after I departed from HP in 2008. Looking back, there was one specific program within the "What do you have to say?" campaign that is a good example of a program that activated discover, empower, and connect in a marketing program and generated impressive early results as a consequence: the Project Direct program.

The Project Direct program was the combined brainchild of HP's media agency (then Zenith Media), a creative agency (Goodby, Silverstein & Partners), and Google (who had recently acquired YouTube)

Table 5.1 The Participation Way

Self-Determination Theory Principle (Nouns)	Participation Way (Verbs)	Definition, Explanation, and Marketing Application
Competence The "accumulated result of one's interactions with the environment." The reward for competency-motivated behavior is the associated feeling that results from feeling capable about what we are doing. These feelings seem to result only when one is able to continually stretch his or her capabilities.	**Discover**	**Discover** is about the human desire to continually learn and the satisfaction of becoming competent at something. *Marketing Application:* In what ways are you inviting participants to **discover** more about your product/brand? Are you allowing them to share what they know it with others? Are you providing them with information and support that allows them to become experts about your product and service?
Autonomy Human development can be characterized in terms of movement toward greater autonomy. This generally refers to the need to have control over the environment or outcomes. But this is more about the need to have a choice, than the outcome of the choice itself. It's about the control for the experience of freedom. People need to feel free from dependence on outcomes that are not within their control. Autonomy is powerful because it has the ability to enhance intrinsic motivation and can also enhance the feeling of competence.	**Empower**	Inviting someone to have a meaningful contribution to the product/brand is what the **empower** attribute is all about. *Marketing Application:* Do you invite participants to provide feedback, offer tips and suggestions, and help *create* the product itself? Do you invite their participation in marketing the product/service? The **empower** and **discover** attributes are closely related and intertwined, but together they allow participants to be actively involved and have a meaningful role with the brand.

Self-Determination Theory Principle (Nouns)	Participation Way (Verbs)	Definition, Explanation, and Marketing Application
Relatedness Relatedness is the need to feel connected to others and to be part of something. It helps moderate autonomy and encourages people to accept responsibility for the well-being of others. We can give and accept responsibility, cooperation, compassion, and respect.	**Connect**	Humans love to **connect** with others in meaningful ways. *Marketing Application:* Brands often think of creating environments that allow participants to connect only with the brand itself—which is often superficial. As a brand, do you remember that you are also a *participant* and connect with other participants in this way? Do you build environments that allow participants to foster relationships with other participants who may share the same interest? Do you **empower** them to showcase what they have **discovered?**

and was part of the larger "What do you have to say?" campaign. However, it was designed for a specific graphic design audience. The program's initial genesis came about when team members from each agency began working on one of the first integrated marketing programs to appear on YouTube. Of course, Google was eager to prove that there was marketing value on their newly acquired platform.

The idea was to host the first ever international film competition called Project Direct as part of the larger international launch of HP's "What do you have to say?" campaign, described earlier. The program was designed to establish HP's Imaging and Printing Graphics Group as a credible source within the online filmmaking community. Its goal was to help filmmakers better promote and build audiences for their short films by providing an incentive and global stage to show-case their work and to also provide a set of printing tools designed to assist with film promotion. HP created an online community within YouTube to facilitate program participation.

The program was a great example of a "build it and they will come" scenario, and it was overwhelmingly popular. It empowered participants to become involved at the instigation of Jason Reitman, producer of *Juno* and *Thank You for Smoking*. Reitman encouraged participants to create short films that incorporated HP's campaign theme line "What do you have to say?" and a printed photograph. The Project Direct YouTube community judged the more than 600 films that people from across the globe had submitted. Interestingly, only 50 percent of the entries came from inside the United States, and the winner was not from the United States. The winning filmmaker from Brazil received a global home page placement on YouTube, along with a trip to the Sundance Film Festival that included a film screening and meeting with partner Fox Searchlight. Project Direct benefitted HP by providing passionate community members with an opportunity to use HP products and services, including a customized tool allowing participants to create and print a poster promoting their film, all in support of their passion of filmmaking. At the contest's conclusion in November, HP unveiled a way for participants and the wider YouTube community to take the promotion of their own videos to the streets with customized iron-on T-shirt designs that used HP's printing technology. Community participants created and printed more than 20,000 T-shirt designs alone. The marketing team carefully thought through the actions they wanted participants to take at every stage of the program.

All of the agencies supporting HP's various marketing disciplines took part in the program creation. The Zenith Media team worked on a YouTube media channel sponsorship, supporting content integration, and on a display ad campaign. HP's search firm Performics developed an associated paid search program so that it could be found and helped drive traffic back to the social experience. The team at Goodby, Silverstein & Partners developed all creative materials. The integrated team of individuals involved operated seamlessly as one team in the collaborative effort. This was rare at the time, given the organizational silos and individual budgets inside of HP. Yet individuals from different respective agencies banded together to create a program designed for participation. No one asked about "working" or "not-working" dollars or what was "above the line" or "below the line." All were focused on facilitating program participation.

In retrospect, HP's Project Direct program effectively used the interdependent ingredients of the Participation Way:

- **Discover:** Project Direct facilitated a filmmaking environment and hosted a competition with credibility by asking a member of the industry—Jason Reitman—to participate. The community provided an avenue for individuals to learn about the filmmaking craft and for others to share their expertise. Because Reitman was just becoming known, his involvement added credibility and excitement, not to mention an award worth pursuing that was important to the participants because of their passion about the industry. Community members voted on finalists, helping reinforce their filmmaking competence.

- **Empower:** The Project Direct Channel empowered individuals by inviting participants to create and submit their films, allowing everyone to vote, and providing them tangible printing tools that supported their filmmaking passion. Filmmakers then promoted their own films even if they were not a winner or involved in the contest. The community and associated tools helped feed their aspiration and helped them feel in control.

- **Connect:** The Project Direct community encouraged participants to meet others who had a common interest: filmmaking. It wasn't just about connecting with HP; however, program participants unanimously claimed that the program changed their perception of HP.

Project Direct revealed the importance of inspiring participation in marketing programs. It was an early example of the recognition of the value of earned media, that clearly demonstrated it was also a working medium. It provided a way for participants to *discover* more about the product through their passion within their own community in an authentic and transparent manner. It *empowered* individuals to take an active role in the marketing program itself by participating in the contest and voting on the finalists. Finally, it allowed inspiring filmmakers to *connect* with one another and use HP's products and services to reinforce that passion.

By adopting and following a simple equation—Discover + Empower + Connect = Participation—the program experienced global participation that far exceeded HP's expectations. Project Direct garnered more than 10 million visits—more than any other channel that included similar programs on YouTube at the time.

They accomplished this by integrating the Participation Way framework and by fully integrating technology, media, and creative.

There has never been a more important time for marketers to understand participation in today's connected world. Companies that embrace the Participation Way will communicate more effectively with customers and employees, add more value, and compete more effectively. Those who don't will not be able to connect to the next generation of customers. Understanding what motivates individuals to participate is essential to marketing in an environment that is more transparent, personal, social, and communal—and undeniably more participatory.

This chapter provided an overview of the Participation Way formula. Creating programs that use these principles allows participants to *discover, empower,* and *connect*, thereby resulting in increased participation and improved performance.

For simplicity and memorability, the Participation Way method has been shortened into a formula: Discover (D) + Empower (E) + Connect (C) = Participation (P), which results in Performance (2): $D + E + C = P2$. The formula is also an effective reminder that in order to achieve participation, activating the entire formula is required. Removing just one ingredient diminishes the result. It is beneficial to break down each component individually for discussion purposes, which is what we will focus on in the next chapter.

Participant Marketing Summary

1. The Participation Way framework is grounded with three primary objectives:

   a. Simple: The framework should be in an easy-to-understand and easy-to-remember format. Most frameworks should consist of no more than three of anything. A simple approach that is easy to remember, explain, and transfer is crucial.

b. Grounded in science: The goal is to create a framework and associated planning tools to support a movement toward participation.

c. Actionable: Frameworks are great in theory; however, they're valuable only if a marketer can actually *use* them to create meaningful programs. Today, the program starts several months before the launch date, starting with planning; then and the real work begins at launch itself. We now have the measurement tools and processes that enable us to constantly adjust our marketing tactics to drive efficiency and effectiveness, taking advantage of active trends in the marketplace that may or may not be driven by our own program. And we have the ability to respond and adjust to participant actions. A good framework needs to take this into account and aid the marketer all along the way.

2. Although adapted from intrinsic motivation and self-determination theory, the Participation Way framework is designed specifically for marketers. The self-determination principles are nouns that describe a state of the environment, but I think it is important that the Participation Way elements be verbs. This is because the goal of marketing in the Participation Age is to invite, encourage, and nurture participation; therefore, the marketing framework should be grounded in a plan that focuses on motivating participants to *take action*.

3. For simplicity and memorability purposes, the Participation Way has been abbreviated into a formula: Discover (D) + Empower (E) + Connect (C) = Participation (P), which results in Performance (2): D + E + C = P2.

6   D + E + C = P2

Discover

As previously discussed, all three Participation Way principles are intrinsically connected. The goal is not to activate them independently, because focusing on just a single principle limits the marketing program effectiveness. However, practicality in the planning and activation processes requires us to think through and address each individual element independently.

As we know, the Participation Way discover principle comes from the self-determination theory. Digging a little deeper into what this means will help us bring this to life for participants in our marketing programs. We have already discussed how technology has enabled humans' desire and ability to continually learn in unimaginable ways—and at any given moment. As such, the following should be considered when activating the discover principle in a marketing program.

1. Discover "Findability"

Today's participants expect to be able to pick up any device at any time and access the information they are seeking. Therefore, the first order of the discover principle is to make sure your product or service can actually *be found*. This means making every element of information findable—not just what the product is and why it's great, but everything around it. You must make information available about where customers can purchase or see it, hours of operation, customer service and troubleshooting, recommendations, and so forth.

One way to envision findability in today's connected world is to think of two spinning wheels resembling the Wheel of Fortune wheel sitting side by side. See Figure 6.1. The participant is constantly spinning the wheel on the right, using various forms of technology

in an effort to find information about the various product or brand.
The brand manages the wheel on the left, which contains unlimited
amounts of content—both owned and earned—sitting at various
points on the wheel. The brand would like to coordinate its spin to
match up with the customer's inquiries. The goal in today's marketing is to make sure that whenever the participant spins the wheel, the
marketer can respond with the appropriate information. The marketing agency's job is to make sure the wheels match up.

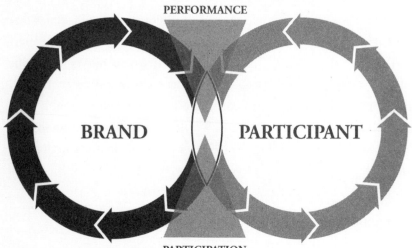

Figure 6.1 Participation Wheel

This means actively managing all programs together, as they are
closely related. For example, both paid and organic search programs
should be managed holistically in an effort to ensure participants
can find the information via search engine—regardless of the device
being used. Search can also be used to gather insight about how to
make a product easier to find. For example, if you are selling tea, you
might notice that in the United Kingdom "afternoon tea" is a popu-
larly searched term and knowing this can assist with not only your
keyword selections but also content development. What *will* change

is level of complexity in search, as participants use tablets, mobile devices, and computers at various times of the day. All these drive us to the same conclusion. It is important to curate earned content that benefits the product, service, and brand on the search engine results page—a new and important consideration when it comes to search.

Marketers sometimes label search to be "old news" and "unexciting" compared with social and mobile marketing. Despite the fact that social has been the golden child of marketing for the past several years, search is still the gold standard for finding information, and that's not going to change anytime soon. If anything, it is even *more* important of a focus now given the interconnectedness between search and social media. Social media, mobile technology, and search have been and will continue to be intrinsically linked. Search drives social media, and social media drives search—and the instances of search will only increase with the number of devices people use and how often they use them. People no longer sit in front of their computers and type something into Google to find it. They search constantly on a number of devices, making it more critical than ever to run programs across devices and platforms. Finally, the Gen Yers who are entering the workforce—and quickly becoming the desired customer for most brands—grew up with search. They expect it to work on every device.

Discover also means ensuring that participants can actively manage and share owned content assets. An example of this is ensuring that they can easily access, save, and share website assets. For example, home furnishing chain Pottery Barn recently posted this on its Facebook Timeline to its fans: "Do you love to pin? We do! We've made it easier than ever to pin our photos. The pin it button is now on every page of our site. Happy pinning!" They are, of course, referring to social media site Pinterest, a perfect findability tool for the discover principle. Pinterest is the fastest-growing social media website in Internet history, even faster than Facebook. It's the third most popular social network in the United States. It launched in March 2010 but really gained momentum during the latter part of 2011. According to Experian's Digital Marketer Trend and Benchmark Report, Pinterest had more than 21 million visits the last week of January 2011. This is 30 times the number of visitors in July 2011; this is the fastest any website in history has reached 10 million visitors. Yet despite the site's popularity and exponential growth, brands have been slow to embrace Pinterest, mostly because there is no way to purchase media on Pinterest and the company has yet to develop its monetization model.

Pinterest is somewhat of an online version of a personal bulletin board. People use it to categorize and organize items they find on the web and to share those items and boards with others. Participants can create their own boards with any theme they choose, such as gardening, architecture, hairstyles, or couches. Then participants can "pin" an image or web page using the link to their board, allowing them to store it. For instance, my daughter has created a wedding board that she uses to store images of favorite dresses, bouquets, colors, invitations, shoes, and so on. She also adds captions or comments about what she likes or wants to use it for. The concept is better than a bridal magazine, because it's personal—filled with only the items *she* likes. My generation created wedding books by clipping from magazines and pasting them into a notebook. Gen Yers are actively collecting and sharing content in new and creative ways.

Pinterest is a perfect forum for discoverability and is a particularly valuable tool for brands trying to reach female participants who like to share their choices with others. And since women represent 85 percent of the buying power in the United States, this is relevant for most brands. At the time of publication, 80 percent of Pinterest's users were women, and the site is currently responsible for more than 4 percent of all referral traffic on the Internet. This is due partially to the fact that participants can easily repin items from other users' boards and like or comment on other photos, similar to functionality in Facebook. The repin functionality also ties into the discover principle of finding satisfaction through competency. It is satisfying to have someone else repin something you collected and shared.

Additional data support the notion that Pinterest is beginning to influence purchasing as well. According to BlogHer's annual study on women and social media, 81 percent of the women surveyed trust Pinterest *more* than Facebook or Twitter. As a result, nearly half of the women surveyed bought something based on a Pinterest recommendation, whereas only one-third bought something based on a Facebook recommendation. Smart brands such as Pottery Barn are leveraging the power of Pinterest to allow participants to discover and share their products. Promoting products and services is less of a concern in an environment like Pinterest, because participants have embraced the idea that Pinterest can be a shopping companion—and many retail clients have found success in using it this way. Even car companies like Volkswagon use the site to help participants discover and use product imagery. In fact, Volkswagon has 18 Pinterest boards: one for each car model.

2. Discover Relevant Content

Humans have an innate desire to continually and progressively learn more. Although this has remained relatively constant for thousands of years, the desire to learn *right here, right now* is a relatively recent phenomenon. In the Participation Age, humans expect to be able to immediately turn to the computer on their desk—or the one in their pocket—to access more information about something relevant to them at the very moment it's relevant. It might be more detailed information about a product or service, side effects of a medication their doctor just prescribed, or a current event they heard mentioned on the radio. The challenge for marketers is to provide these information-hungry participants with continually relevant information in a timely manner and with context. From an owned content standpoint, this means constantly creating and curating content to satisfy this need. It also requires making this content easy to find, as previously discussed. Data-informed marketing will also improve context in the future.

3. Discover Recognition

You might think of discovering recognition as *how* to empower participation, which is something gaming companies understand very well. It's no accident that games are designed with stages that enable individuals to advance in skill levels and that they provide rich, rewarding feedback along the way. It might not seem like traditional marketing to plan programs that are designed to continually reward participants who have competence around a product, service, or brand; however, this is an important contributor to motivating involvement and should therefore be considered if the goal is to inspire participation.

Unfortunately, few brands recognize this attribute, and most fail to create programs with this kind of focus. Some do it for frequent users; after all, reward programs have been around for decades in various forms. I have no idea how many rewards cards I carry in my wallet or membership numbers I keep in my phone, but the traditional format of reward cards is evolving. Many brands today are using the social check-in site Foursquare, which has built-in rewards, as a modern approach to bring reward activities to their marketing programs. Foursquare is a location-based social networking website for mobile devices such as smartphones, and it allows participants to check in at venues using a mobile website, text messaging, or a device-specific application by selecting from a list of nearby places. Location is based on GPS hardware in the mobile device or network location provided by the application. Users receive points for each check-in and sometimes can earn badges once a specified number of points has been reached. Many businesses, such as restaurants, have embraced the location-based application. It allows participants to interact with their environment, in the real world and in the virtual world, and rewards those who frequently check in by providing them with specific discounts, coupons, or preferential treatment. American Express was one of Foursquare's most prominent early partners. It developed a program that enables cardholders to sync their cards with their Foursquare accounts to redeem savings by checking in at a variety of restaurants, clothing stores, and sporting goods retailers.

Of course, competence recognition is trickier than just implementing a loyalty program. Remember, the goal is to reward someone for knowledge and expertise, which could—but doesn't always—come from increased use. There are ways to do this by letting customers submit their own knowledge and information, thereby allowing them to achieve levels that unlock additional information not available to those who haven't shared as much. Another tactic is to simply allow them to supply their knowledge and expertise and let others view it in the form of reviews, ratings, community customer service, and so on. This is also satisfying because it reinforces the feeling of competency.

In summary, the discover principle is about making sure your product, service, and brand can be found and continually creating and curating relevant content to help participants feel more competent about the product or service or brand.

Participant Marketing Summary: Activating the Discover Principle

1. Discover findability. Today's participants expect to be able to pick up any device at any time and access the information they are seeking. Therefore, the first order of the discover principle is to make sure your product or service can actually *be found*. This

means making every element of information findable—not just what the product is and why it's great, but everything around it. You must make information available about where customers can purchase or see it, hours of operation, customer service and troubleshooting, recommendations, and so forth.

2. Discover relevant content. Humans have an innate desire to continually learn and find out more information. Although this has remained relatively constant for thousands of years, the desire to learn *right here, right now* is a relatively recent phenomenon. In the Participation Age, humans are able to immediately turn to the computer on their desk—or the one in their pocket—to access information about something applicable to them at the very moment it's relevant.

3. Discover recognition. You might think of discovering recognition as *how* to empower participation, which is something gaming companies understand very well. It's no accident that games are designed with stages that enable individuals to advance to a number of skill levels and provide rich, rewarding feedback along the way. It might not seem like traditional marketing to plan programs that are designed to continually reward participants who have competence around a product, service, or brand; however, this is an important contributor to motivating participation and should therefore be considered if the goal is to inspire participation.

7 D + E + C = P2

Empower

Empower is one of those words that is often overused and some-times misinterpreted, so bear with me for a bit as I explain the choice to use this as the active verb for the Participation Way that correlates with autonomy. Like *engage, empower* is a word for which everyone has a different definition—and therefore a word that's easily misunderstood.

However, *empower* is a good choice because of the strong cor-relation to *power*. As discussed previously, there is no question about the undeniable power participants wield in today's marketplace. Consequently, this ingredient of the Participation Way formula is particularly potent since it also ties to the emotional component of competence, which, as we already discussed, directly enhances intrin-sic motivation overall. Sociologists have suggested that this "auton-omy or empowerment drive"—that is, individuals' desire to manage their environment and outcomes—has always been present, with or without technology. However, I believe that now more than ever, people have far-reaching expectations about what their relationships should be like with the brands that provide the products and services they use. Marketers have always acknowledged the contribution of word of mouth in how individuals learn from others' positive and negative experiences with a product or brand. Now, technology has armed these participants with communication tools and connection to networks that enable them to broadcast this information far and wide—allowing them to assemble an army of other individuals with the same sentiment. So, in a way, the amplification of word of mouth has grown exponentially. Data are also confirming this fact as market-ers begin to understand and correlate the actions associated with the complexity of networks and the impact this has on brands from prod-uct choices to reputation management.

A recent Performics research study found that 32 percent of respondents believe their voice can make a difference with a brand. This means they believe that they can get the brand's attention about the issue and they expect the brand to take an appropriate action— right away. The noteworthy distinction is the expectation concerning response time. The computers that participants now carry in their pockets make it easy for them to communicate a good or bad brand experience in real time, and they expect an immediate response.

As referenced in earlier chapters, a number of studies have indicated autonomy or empowerment to be more about the need to have a choice than the outcome of the choice itself. In essence, it is all about having control and desiring to experience freedom. In fact, a number of studies determined that people do not always want to control their outcomes; they simply want to choose whether or not to be in control. This ties back also to the immediacy of the response. This is crucial for marketers to understand as we begin to apply the empower principle to the Participation Way. The core tenant here is that people today expect to have a choice—regardless of whether they choose to exercise it or not. And, they expect it right now. Although the "have a choice" component may always have been a factor, participants are now empowered to make their voice heard instantaneously if they feel that brands aren't acknowledging them. Brands historically have relished controlling the message in both content and distribution. They orchestrated every campaign moment to manage how, when, and to whom they communicated the message, and they never considered reciprocal communication. In reality, there is no going back. Control no longer really exists. Reciprocity and changed expectations are here to stay.

Despite the need to acknowledge this reality, empowering participants is likely the element in the Participation Way formula that marketers fear most, for all the reasons we have discussed. I understand and empathize with this, especially given the amount of pressure most

organizations feel to deliver tangible business results. Marketers have
all heard about and are repeatedly reminded of the social marketing
horror stories in which companies have allowed customers or potential customers to "control" the situation. As with most circumstances,
the bad news spreads faster and reaches farther than the good.

It doesn't really matter if you decide to "give" your customers
control; in truth they already have it, and brands have already lost
it. Countless companies are hanging on to a false sense of security
that no longer exists. However, there is an opportunity to embrace
the situation and develop programs that empower individuals to
act on behalf of the product, service, or brand. A number of studies
show that, when done authentically and transparently, participants
embrace this role. This is especially true for Gen Y participants, who
have different definitions and expectations of advertising in general.
Furthermore, there are smart tools and tactics available for empowering participants, which we discuss in the following sections.

1. Begin with an Active Understanding of the Participants

At Performics, we use what we call a participation audit, and its role
is to determine the marketing environment and participant mind-set
and motivations that will drive the approach and tactics for empowerment. This foundational stage is critical for all marketing planning
today, particularly in the participative environment. I was keen to
create a new process for program and consumer insight when I left
Hewlett-Packard (HP), during a time when social marketing was
just beginning to gain momentum. The focus group planning tools
we were using—and still are using, in many cases—seem archaic.
They are slower and more limited in the number of worldwide individuals they can survey than are the currently available social listening tools and techniques, which are far more authentic and wide
reaching. Marketing strategy has historically relied on developing

communication strategies that came from the concept of positioning, and positioning was often determined by using qualitative focus
group planning to determine the emotional benefits.

The idea behind creating new methods for participation planning was to replicate the approach from Jonathan Gutman's original
benefit laddering techniques based on a book he authored in 1982.
Mr. Gutman is currently a professor of marketing and chairman at
the Whittemore School of Business and Economics at the University
of New Hampshire in Durham. His marketing methods have long
been influential in using focus groups to create marketing messages
for a number of years. The methods themselves still have some relevance today; however, the difference is that social listening tools
are used as a more accurate and timely substitute for focus group
feedback. Furthermore, what is gathered today should be less about
gathering information to create a message and more about gathering
information to inspire participation. Gutman emphasized the value
in laddering product benefits because of the importance of product
positioning for communications planning and message development.
Historically, positioning required that brands determine exactly what
to communicate in an effort to persuade consumers to achieve the
desired response over time. The focus group research methods allowed
marketers to determine which product attributes "laddered up" to a
compelling emotional benefit that would elicit the desired response.

For example, if your laundry soap cleaned clothes just as effectively as any other laundry soap products could, product benefits
around cleanliness likely weren't very effective due to the lack of dif-
ferentiation in that positioning. In addition, logical product benefits
often weren't persuasive because they were missing the emotional
component about why laundry soap was so compelling. So Gutman
championed a process that would ladder from the product attribute
of cleanliness to the emotional benefit that surrounded cleanliness.
He focused on elements such as how clean clothes smelled, which

then tied the product to something more powerful, such as feeling free because you feel clean, feeling connected to a particular movie star after learning he or she uses the product, or believing that the clean, fresh scent made you irresistible to a potential partner. Tapping into the senses has also long been known to evoke powerful emotions that can be used to create persuasive marketing messages.

Gutman's means-ends theory centers on the connections among the product's attributes (the "means"), the consumer advantages (the "consequences") provided by the product attribute, and the personal values (the "ends") that the consequences reinforce. In other words, it was thought that consumers seek certain attributes in products and that these attributes lead to certain consequences (or benefits). He believed that if the consequences mattered to consumers, they would learn to choose products and services that possess those attributes that lead to the relevant advantages.

Because of the focus on message persuasion, this concept very much resembles the mechanistic motivation theory discussed in Chapter 4, in which the human organism is thought to be passive and led by the surrounding environment. It is not consistent with the organismic theory in the Participation Age, where humans initiate the behavior and control the environment—which isn't passive at all. Today's participants do not want to be led to do the right thing over time. Therefore, we have to change not only the way in which we gather the information but what we do with it as well. That said, it's vital that marketers understand the linkages between product attributes, their consequences, and their ultimate participant "values" or benefits if they want to empower a participant to take a specific action on behalf of the brand.

The traditional focus group technique required an interviewer who could ask probing questions without sounding obtrusive or judgmental. The greater the interviewer's skills in eliciting responses, the richer the output of the research would be. And although the technique is still used widely in qualitative focus group discussions, results seem to be applied only to one-way message creation. There is no question that I have gathered valuable information from the various focus group sessions I've watched. I just believe we are ready for a new approach that sincerely taps into participants' hearts and minds, with an ear toward learning what inspires them to take action and using the new social tools and technology we now have at our disposal.

Participation planning and the participation audit are both methods that we have used quite successfully to gain insight before beginning a campaign. The audit is a process whereby a strategic map is created that contains *what* information individuals are saying about a product, service, or brand; *where* they are saying it (Is it occurring on an "earned" environment or "owned" environment?); and *when* these conversations are happening (Are there specific events that cause participation to occur that the brand might not have considered?). Marketers can mine the "what" section for product information as well as emotional attribute information. Both are relevant in helping develop programs designed for participants to discover as much about the product or service in order to feel competent about their ability to make a decision.

To gather this information, social listening tools are utilized that enable direct tool access, such as Nielsen BuzzMetrics. This means the need to have a seat in the tool directly enables live information gathering where the user can follow threads, similar to what formerly occurred in a focus group session. Nielsen BuzzMetrics is just one of many tools currently available in the marketplace. We have found it important to continually evaluate social listening providers, given the number of tools being added to the market and the highly competitive nature of the listening space. This enables the user to manually pull and clean data, crucial in developing an audit. Most brands actually pay for a social listening service. This is great, and we recommend our brands do this. However, the listening reports created are generally not a substitute for a participation audit, nor do they serve the same purpose. Although we've found many brands that pay for and receive regular reports, and some find this information valuable, we also know that many brands are simply overwhelmed with the information they are receiving. As a result, they often fail to use this insightful information to plan or change their marketing programs, which is, of course, the whole point of social listening in the first place! Most of these providers also focus on sentiment, which is a fine attribute but not specific enough to drive strategy.

The process of creating a participation audit is still quite manual; electronic tools are only part of the process. The real insight still occurs from highly skilled planners who compile the information into a strategic format, similar to the traditional focus group moderator. Many social listening providers claim they provide aggregation, cleaning, analysis, and insight of the data they've pulled from public social platforms data, including social networks, blogs, boards, groups, and so on. Although this meets the need for aggregation, this is only the first step and it's unusual to find a service who aggregates social data and combines it with search data—another powerful source of perceptions and insights.

I set out to pilot the participation audit several years ago, when every brand wanted to do "something social" in marketing. Having keen insight into social environments is critical to brands. The party analogy was used often to warn brands about the hazards of entering the social sphere: You don't have an official invitation; you don't know who is going to be there or how everyone will be dressed. And you don't know what conversations will be taking place. Yet as a brand, you expect to attend and dominate the entire conversation. This is probably not going to go very well.

One of my favorite and well-known examples is the program General Motors (GM) introduced in the spring of 2006, crowdsourcing ads for the Chevy Tahoe. (Although a bit dated, this example is insightful because it's easier to look backward to recognize mistakes.)

GM was very early in empowering participants when it created a site where anyone could create their own Tahoe ads. But what happened was not at all what GM expected. Participants created some of the funniest (perhaps not amusing to GM) anti-Chevy parodies ever seen on the Internet—and the campaign is still considered one of the most colossal social media failures of all time.

GM should be credited for being brave enough to embrace the empower principle at such an early stage in the social media space. It was, however, most unfortunate for them, as the campaign launched at a time when the green movement was riding a strong wave of popularity. Oil prices were beginning to climb, and the United States was early into the war in Iraq, viewed by some as a battle for petroleum and already taking a toll on American morale. Hurricane Katrina had taken place during this time and consequently put global climate change on the front pages of all the newspapers and front and center in people's minds. A big SUV like the Tahoe was a perfect target for some anger, and it got plenty, courtesy of many outrageous user-generated ads. (For those who don't remember, a collection from the ads can be found on Flickr and there are video mashups on YouTube.)

A participation audit could have helped GM immensely—first, to potentially prevent the unexpected public outpouring of negative sentiment. Had GM been able to see the aggregated conversations that individuals were having about vehicles, they might have been able to detect early sentiment regarding their brand, large vehicles in general, and fuel efficiency. This might have at least prepared them for the response to the marketing campaign, and it might have altered their approach. But, even if they had gathered the information and not created a marketing program at all and had instead had used the data in a way that affected not only their marketing plans but also their product development plans, imagine what might have transpired then—both for marketing and product development. What if they had listened to the public sentiment about concern over fuel economy and global climate change—and responded by developing smaller, more fuel-efficient vehicles before their competitors did? Even if they had not gone that far, what if they had asked people what types of vehicles they would like to see and offered to involve them in the development ideation? I often wonder if this could that have changed the bankruptcy chain of events or had an impact on the entire auto industry. Although there certainly were not as many listening tools in 2006, search trends were accessible and could have also provided valuable insight.

The obvious premise here is that it's more important to understand participants' hearts and minds now than it ever has been before. And because both of these change continually, staying on top of the emotional values important to participants is more crucial than ever. Traditional tools are just not sufficient for this. The core value of Gutman's approach is not irrelevant; it just needs to be modified for today's environment.

2. Decide on the Desired Participant Action

Decide what action you want participants to take before developing the marketing program. Although this might seem obvious, it is often missing completely from marketing planning because marketers are focused on the message, not the actions. Traditional marketing tools are designed around what we want people to think, not what we want them to do. This approach also ties back to brands' and companies' fear of relinquishing control, which often causes brands to avoid launching a listening program altogether. An active conversation about what actions you want participants to take can be quite rewarding psychologically, because it actually helps marketers gain a sense of control. This also sets the foundation for measurement. When planning measurement for HP's "What do you have to say?" printing campaign, I worked with my agency partners to develop a comprehensive measurement standardization approach. It specifically outlined the success parameters of the campaign, beginning with participant actions. As a result, we had a rigorous discussion and were able to categorize every action that then drove the standardization of critical interactions to develop each marketing asset and program. For example, the top priority actions were to register, save a project, and print. We created the assets so that we had tagging capability to track each of these actions. We also had a secondary set of actions that were a lower priority. These included selecting links to HP.com or learning more about a product or service. We then assigned a measurement value to each of these actions (to be discussed in greater detail in Chapter 10). The opportunities to use data to better inform marketing decisions are unlimited today, especially if marketers are willing to have an open mind about the process—and not focus on creating a dashboard only rather than including true measurement and return on investment (ROI) tracking. This brings me to my next point.

3. Recognize the Importance of Measurement and ROI

Although these two elements aren't often closely tied to actions, they should be. Actions are the manifestation of participation. The empowerment discussion is a great opportunity to have a robust discussion about how to measure your marketing program. The beautiful thing about focusing on action is that actions are measurable. Many social networks, such as Facebook, for example, like to control the measurement within their own walled garden; however, it can be challenging to piece together all the measured components and understand a program's true end-to-end impact. Regardless, it's still valuable to have a healthy discussion about what actions you are asking of participants. Even if you don't really know what actions will occur, develop a hypothesis and then prove it wrong or right by using measurement processes and tools. Do not let a lack of historical benchmarks be an excuse not to have this conversation or not to have measurement at all. Many tools can help you make an educated guess, and the great thing about the new marketing approach is that you can easily adjust it if it's not performing as you expected.

Finally, realize that embracing the empower principle is a philosophical adjustment for marketers. The whole notion of empowering someone on your behalf requires that you give him or her equal standing in the relationship—a significant mind-set shift for most brands. Although this philosophy is core to the Participation Way, in general, when you are at the step of looking to empower participants, it is a good time to do a self-health check. Are you asking participants to do something you wouldn't do yourself? Are you, the brand, acting as a participant or as a bully in the program? Do you have the right governance models operating within your organization to manage the program's potential outcomes? Almost all organizations have silos that prevent marketing effectiveness, and empowering participants will likely effect more than just the marketing department. Participants don't care if customer service and marketing don't talk with one another or report into the same departmental lead in the organization. They simply expect the brand to act as one unit. Therefore, having systems in place to compensate for organizational dysfunction is a great idea and is what governance programs are all about.

Empower participants to drive your marketing program. Marketers tend to focus only on extending the message through "viral" tactics. This limits the opportunity without embracing the transparent, authentic participative environment. Integration no longer happens as the sole responsibility of the marketer, nor is it just about message consistency. Integration in the Participation Age is about empowering others to drive integration for you and enabling them to add value with content, insight, and opinion along the way. The marketers' goal is to keep the momentum going and to tap into participants' networks—something we'll discuss more thoroughly as we move into the connect stage (discussed in the next chapter).

Participant Marketing Summary

Empowering participants is about giving them the freedom to make choices. Participants do not always want to control their outcomes; they simply want to choose whether or not to be in control. This is crucial for marketers to understand as we begin to apply the empower principle to the Participation Way.

1. Begin with an understanding of the participants and their environments. You can do this by conducting a participation audit to determine *what* they're saying, *where* participation is occurring, and *when* the events driving participation activities are happening.

2. Decide what action you want participants to take before developing the marketing program. Although this might seem obvious, it is often missing completely from marketing planning because marketers are focused on the message, not the actions. Traditional marketing tools are designed around what we want people to think, not what we want them to do. This approach also ties back to brands' and companies' fear of relinquishing control, which often causes brands to avoid launching a listening program altogether.

3. Recognize the importance of measurement and ROI. Measurement and ROI are not often closely tied to actions, but they should be because actions are, in essence, the manifestation of participation.

8 D + E + C = P2

Connect

As we learn more about the new connected world in which we live, we understand more clearly the profound affect individuals have on one another for even the most basic of choices. We live in a highly connected, highly networked world—and part of marketing's new responsibility is to help facilitate and enable these connections. The emphasis to connect comes from the relatedness attribute of the self-determination theory and refers to the need to feel connected to others. As mentioned in earlier chapters, humans are social creatures with an intrinsic need to be a part of something bigger, and this includes relationships. Recent technology obviously helps facilitate this by allowing individuals with like minds and similar interests to connect anytime, anywhere, virtually or in person. Connecting in this way lets people feel as though they belong to a larger community.

Companies that are marketing in the Participation Age must connect by actively considering what relationship their product, service, or brand has with participants in an authentic and transparent manner, of course. They must also determine how to further support participants' desire to connect with other participants. Products, services, and brands are passion points around which participants like to connect, so actively managing community activities as part of marketing is what the connect element in the Participation Way is all about. Consider the following when activating the connect element in a marketing program.

1. A Brand Is a Participant

Connection, in a broader sociological construct, helps moderate autonomy, encourages symmetry, and balances our individual viewpoint. We can apply this to a brand perspective as well. The connect principle acts as perspective and a reminder that the brand itself must also act accordingly to participant rules. The product, service, or brand is not the center of the universe. It is a brand's responsibility to genuinely accept responsibility for other participants' well-being. They cannot just claim to do this, but must demonstrate it so as to balance the brand-centric point of view.

Of course, actually doing this requires planning, coordination, and a willingness to develop a relationship with current and potential customers. This may again require working on internal organizational plans and instituting governance programs to help create processes to facilitate relationships.

Let's look at a specific example of a company that experienced some connecting challenges and eventually overcame them. LEGO has been a popular toy and household name for more than 70 years. My brother, now in his mid-40s, grew up with LEGOs. He wasn't just a customer as a child; he continues to be passionate about the brand and will probably always be an advocate. In recent years, LEGO has fully embraced the importance of connecting in the overall marketing mix and is now seeing the benefits to their bottom line. I recently attended a Digiday Conference, where an individual in LEGO's Consumer Marketing Group discussed how the company's marketing group is actively motivating their loyal fans to spread LEGO love—and thereby shifting their marketing strategy holistically by motivating participation.

For decades, LEGO, like most companies, did not recognize the importance of tapping into the connect element of the Participation Way. They did not have support programs that allowed customers to provide suggestions and ideas. Rather, they conducted business in a manner that had really been successful for many years by creating products they believed consumers wanted.

This marking approach appeared to work fine until the holiday season of 1999, when three of LEGO's largest distributors—Walmart,

Target, and Toys R Us—informed the toy maker that it had lost touch with its customer base. Many kids, like my brother, had grown up on LEGOs; many were now adults and having children of their own. These adult LEGO fans were still passionate about the brand; they were forming their own discussion groups online, creating their own online marketplaces to buy and sell LEGO products, sharing photos of LEGO designs, and even discussing new product ideas. Some of this activity was even generating press coverage, and all of it was happening without LEGO's support or endorsement. The brand continued to insist that their product was a toy created for kids and that adults were not their primary customer—or worthy of their attention.

This is another scenario where a participation audit could have offered a substantial advantage. LEGO might have discovered what kind of participation was occurring with regard to the brand, where it was happening, and what type of events were driving energy around participation. In the past several years, LEGO has transformed its marketing organization, including creating an internal, full-service agency whose role is to develop original content and participant experiences. LEGO recognized in the early stages that a shift had occurred and realized that it had a choice to either embrace it or continue to manage marketing in a traditional manner. LEGO understands that it needs to not only act as a participant but also facilitate the community of passionate LEGO participants.

2. Participant-to-Participant Connections Are Equally Important

It isn't necessary for every marketing program to have a complex community built specifically for every program. However, brands should thoroughly consider how they enable participants to connect—both to the brand and to other participants. This adds a dimension to the marketing program that most brands frequently don't bother to consider. It can be very valuable to think about the connect principle for individual marketing tactics.

For example, are you thinking about applying connect as part of your search program? Does your search program include ways for participants to connect with others who are passionate about the product, service, or brand? This enables participants to find other passionate participants. In the case of LEGO, the turning point came when the company created several programs specifically designed to connect participants with both the brand and other participants. The first program created was the LEGO Ambassador Program. Made up of 40 LEGO fans ranging in age from 19 to 65 who reside around the world, the Ambassador program is designed to provide LEGO with ideas and advice.

Individuals from the marketing team communicate with this group more or less daily to discuss different themes or ideas or to brainstorm. The ambassadors report on discussions via blogs, create picture galleries, and continue the talks with their local LEGO group members. The Ambassador Program has allowed LEGO to open up a channel for conversation and invite participation with its most passionate group of customers.

Another example of a program LEGO created to connect with participants is the Click Community. In 2011, LEGO made its official venture into social media with LEGO Click, a collaborative website that encourages fans, artists, designers, and inventors to share their own LEGO creations. LEGO Click visitors can also read recent tweets about LEGO or download the free LEGO Photo iPhone application that transforms photos into LEGO creations. Users can also log in to the site using their Twitter account and fly a mini LEGO man around the screen. The LEGO Click Community formalized a new network for fans that encourages participation and conversation. LEGO has harnessed this participation by making it easy to for participants to share content, resulting in content amplification. LEGO has enjoyed tremendous revitalized success in the past few years as a result of their new approach to marketing. LEGO now clearly understands and is actively connecting with its participant base. Perhaps even more important, the brand has fundamentally changed its approach to doing business by embracing participant marketing as core to not only marketing but product development, distribution, and customer service.

The LEGO example illustrates how the connect element of the Participation Way opens the door to a new form of customer relationship management. It's a fundamental shift in philosophy and begins when brands accept responsibility and invite cooperation, while keeping compassion and respect top of mind; it, along with the discover and empower elements, ignites participation.

Participant Marketing Summary

1. The emphasis to connect comes from the relatedness attribute of the self-determination theory and refers to the need to feel connected to others. As mentioned previously, humans are social creatures with an intrinsic need to be a part of something bigger, including relationships with other humans. Recent technology obviously helps facilitate this by allowing individuals with like minds and similar interests to connect anytime, anywhere. Connecting in this way lets people feel as though they belong to a larger community.

2. A brand is a participant. In a broader sociological construct, connection helps moderate autonomy, encourages symmetry, and balances our individual point of view. From a brand standpoint, the connect principle acts as perspective and a reminder that the brand itself must also act according to participant rules.

3. Participant-to-participant connections are equally important. It isn't necessary for every marketing program to have a complex community built specifically for every program. However, brands should thoroughly consider how they enable participants to connect—both to the brand and to other participants. This adds a dimension to the marketing program that most brands frequently don't bother to consider. It can be very valuable to think about the connect principle for individual marketing tactics.

9 D + E + C = P2

Participation

Participation is powerful. The active process of people joining, sharing, connecting, and engaging manifests in many different forms. The new forms of self-expression and creativity that technology has unleashed have brought with them behavioral changes, as well an evolving throng of new expectations. The examples around us are plentiful, thought provoking, and, in some cases, even mind-blowing.

YouTube is only 13 years young, and despite the fact that Google acquired it in 2006, it still employs fewer than 1,000 individuals. As it has evolved over the years, YouTube has increasingly become a real-time reflection of what is happening in the real world. According to the company's Trends manager, Kevin Allocca, "Nearly everything that happens in the world plays out, in some way, on YouTube." YouTube Trends tracks this phenomenon by posting a scrolling list of the top videos of live events as they are happening. From earthquakes to sporting events, elections to riots, millions of participants are capturing live events as they occur and sharing them with the world. The rise of mobile has had a dramatic effect as more and more participants carry a video camera in their pockets, capturing even more events in real time. This differs dramatically from having to wait for newspapers to receive "official" reports of the day's or week's events. In fact, more and more "official" newsmakers are setting information free in real time in order to then receive additional information, allowing stories to be more timely and accurate. For example, newspapers are releasing information as it happens, so news never has a final deadline as it did in the past. Furthermore, news organizations are asking for participant input, and individuals who witnessed events are commenting in real time. Award-winning journalist Simon Rogers, author of *Facts Are Sacred* and editor of the *Guardian*'s Datablog, discussed recently how major publishers, including the *Guardian*, are using data to explain live news in powerful new ways. YouTube is certainly a reflection of this.

Sixty hours of video is uploaded to YouTube every minute, which means that every day of real time contains nearly a year of YouTube time. In 2011, a film called *Life in a Day* was released at the Sundance Film Festival. The movie was a result of producers Ridley Scott and Kevin Macdonald's curating of 4,500 hours of participant-created videos from 192 countries, all captured in a single day. The project itself is a powerful reflection of today's active content-creating participants who are no longer satisfied to simply sit back as passive members of the audience. Rather, these individuals have evolved into creators armed with cameras built into a device that sits in the pocket of 87 percent of the world's population. They expect to immerse themselves in the experience; they want to create, influence, add to it, subtract from it, and, ultimately, share it with others.

The power of participation is also influencing how Hollywood creates content. YouTube is at the forefront of this, seeking to leverage its heritage of curating original, user-generated content and transferring Participation Age tenets to professional programming. YouTube has brought on an impressive list of content producers that includes big names like comedienne and television star Amy Poehler, sought-after physician/speaker/writer Deepak Chopra, and musical and acting superstar Madonna—in addition to countless other traditional media pioneers hoping to be the first revolutionists pioneering the future of participative media. Not to be left out, Yahoo! is also creating original content that is designed for and will be released only online. *Electric City*, an animated series created by and starring Tom Hanks, was released last summer; Yahoo! touts it as the web's first international blockbuster premium series. It's one of a handful of new ventures the 17-year-old web company is preparing to introduce as content designed for the future for the world's largest audience with the participant in mind. Not only is this content designed for digital environments first, but producers are making real-time adjustments to the content based on participant feedback, transitioning the medium from a passive one to one that is increasingly reciprocal and interactive.

Video and television are not the only examples of media experiencing a transition. Even live Broadway productions are seeking innovative ways to immerse their audiences and involve them in the theatrical experience in a way that satisfies their desire to become a part of the production itself.

The 2011 Broadway production of *Sleep No More* describes itself as an "immersive theater installation." The play, an adaptation of Shakespeare's *Macbeth*, takes place in three abandoned warehouses on West 27th Street in New York City and involves participants in a way formerly unimaginable by theatergoers. Upon entering the "theater," individuals receive a mask to wear and instantly become part of the production. This might include running up and down stairs and through darkly lit, furniture-cluttered rooms and corridors. They are also empowered to move freely at their own pace or even explore parts of the building on their own, choosing where to go, what to see, and when to see it. The production has no seats, or stage, or any of the other classical theatrical setups that a traditional audience might expect.

Each participant ends up having a unique experience that plunges him or her deeper into the actual story line, allowing that person to actually feel every heart-pounding, mysterious sensation within the story, rather than just watching the production from a distance. The play's production company, called Punchdrunk, has created a modern example how traditional media forms are embracing a more deeply participative experience due to culturally changing expectations. Punchdrunk senior producer Colin Nightingale started out his career as a DJ, but 10 years ago he decided to search for something "different and exciting and relevant for our time." That's when he encountered Punchdrunk, and he said it just felt like he had found it. "People have accepted that they are in control, and you can't take that back," Nightingale said. "We have to keep an eye on what's happening, but for us the motivation to evolve is always from an artistic desire to ensure that we create relevant and exciting experiences for our audiences, rather than any calculated desire to keep up with the changing environment."

The British company has been inviting traditional audiences to become participants in a variety of projects over the past 12 years and been rewarded with unquestionable success. Despite the fact that the production of *Sleep No More* has never been advertised, every show has sold out.

Punchdrunk is not just a theater production company. They've also produced participative marketing experiences for brands like Belgian brewery Stella Artois and French fashion house Louis Vuitton to create experiential product launches in the United Kingdom. The Stella work—productions called "The Night Chauffeur" and the "The Black Diamond"—were both dramatic and yet classic film noir plots full of emotion that involved the participant in the story.

Punchdrunk now has a grant from Nesta to partner with MIT's Media Lab to experiment in adding digital elements to the *Sleep No More* experience. The study will likely demonstrate the thin line between the virtual and the digital world, as well as the expectations around how digital fits into our real-life experiences.

Brands that embrace participation frequently enjoy a significant increase in overall short-term marketing effectiveness. In the long term, they get a head start in adapting to the new media culture. The objective is to adapt ahead of the curve, before competitors do. Marketing, however, is already behind the curve, because the shift happened some time ago.

Despite the connection between marketing and entertainment, most marketers cannot envision creating an environment like

Sleep No More. In an effort to get advertisers to think differently about this new media landscape, Google is innovating in creative ways beyond the YouTube example. In producing Project Re: Brief, Google harnessed a traditional medium (television) and powerful pop culture ads from the past. They had the original ad creators recreate the spots using technology and participatory culture ethos. They even brought in the original creative geniuses: Bob Pasqualina, Howie Cohen, Amil Gargano, Harvey Gabor, and Paula Green to reimagine the ad conceptual experiences.

Project Re: Brief fashioned new ad experiences based on old ad television spots for Coca-Cola, Avis, Volvo, and Alka-Seltzer. The end result is a visual representation of the opportunity of the future of advertising revolutionized for the Participation Age. The new Coke concept literally empowers participants to connect with other Coke-loving participants around the globe. The original campaign, "Buy the world a Coke and keep it company," is actually brought to life in a new technology-enabled manner. A network-connected banner empowers participants by letting them record a message that they can send to a vending machine screen to someone elsewhere in the world. The underlying concept remains the same, but creating an environment that uses technology to empower and connect individuals makes it even more relevant to today's expectations.

Recollecting the original Alka-Seltzer television spot featuring Ralph, who sat miserably on the side of his bed in his slippers and profoundly exclaimed, "I can't believe I ate the whole thing," the new Re: Briefed ad enables participants to discover more about Ralph's whole story, providing very specific details to what actually happened to get Ralph to "eat the whole thing." The brilliance comes about when each prior fact is revealed in a customized manner to the participant viewing the ad, including time, location, weather, and even nuanced details such as specific community events. For example, let's say that I watched the ad from my laptop in Boise, Idaho. The experience would unfold for me in Boise, with Boise's current weather and actual activities that happened that day. In essence, the participant is now really sitting in Ralph's slippers, discovering what Ralph experienced and becoming part of the story with the product and the brand—through a whole new participatory dimension.

Brands that harness the power of the Participation Way can motivate participants to take action on behalf of and as part of the brand. The keys are to create an experience that taps into all three elements of the Participation Way formula—discover, empower, and connect—and to determine precisely which actions you want participants to take.

Marketers must truly understand and embrace the participant and the experience; the goal shouldn't be to devise a trick to create something that becomes "viral." This is an important distinction because creating something viral involves being clever and—to a certain extent—sneaky and inauthentic. The examples mentioned previously are authentic and upfront in that they explicitly ask for individuals to participate. In doing so, they make the experience unique to each one of them. It's still important to have a creative idea that draws users in and entertains them in a thoughtful way that benefits both participants and the brand. This was exactly what Google intended to illustrate in Project Re: Brief. Brands that do this well motivate participants to join, share, take part, and connect—actions that ultimately translate into improved performance and marketing effectiveness, which is what we will talk about in the next chapter.

Performance Marketing Summary

1. Brands that harness the power of the Participation Way can motivate participants to take action on behalf of and as part of the brand. The keys are to create an experience that taps into all three elements of the Participation Way formula—discover, empower, and connect—and to determine precisely which actions you want participants to take.

2. Marketers must understand and embrace the participant and the experience; the goal shouldn't be to devise a trick to create something that becomes viral.

3. Brands that do this well motivate participants to join, share, take part, and connect—actions that ultimately translate into improved performance and marketing effectiveness.

10 D + E + C = P2

Performance

Digital technology makes it easier for marketers to determine what does and doesn't work. Some marketers have taken the next step and tied this to evaluate overall marketing return on investment (ROI). Analytics techniques are now available to provide marketers and their agency partners with the marketing effectiveness data in real time. This is both good and bad news for today's marketers.

I thought my job was relatively challenging when I was working in marketing at Hewlett-Packard (HP). However, it now looks pretty simple compared with what's required by today's standards. For most of my years at HP, the majority of our marketing activities and budgets were centered on product launches. We would plan for months to develop all the marketing communications activities leading up to the big launch. In some ways, those days were much easier for marketers because we would all breathe a sigh of relief the day after the launch and then relax for a month or two before ramping up for the next one. We spent more than 80 percent of our budgets in the first three months following the launch date, and generally we didn't even bother to review the campaign's effectiveness until six months later. We usually measured effectiveness in the form of awareness and preference for the product and service, media spend effectiveness, and share of voice compared with that of competitors during that time period. Let's face it: we basically convinced company leadership that we could not absolutely prove or disprove the effectiveness of our marketing spend. In some cases, organizations were able to develop algorithms that they insisted correlated marketing spend directly to sales. In other cases, there was no correlation at all; management teams were simply putting faith in marketing decisions. Regardless, we are now at a turning point for marketing. This is due to the shifting participant expectations, as well as the need to have

more holistic continuous relationships. It is also because the expectations around what data can or cannot demonstrate about marketing
effectiveness ROI are changing how organizational leadership views
marketing performance.

If this isn't complicated enough, today's marketer has an even
more challenging role—for a number of reasons. First, as we have
discussed in earlier chapters, there are fewer resources dedicated to
marketing and digital, despite the increase in digital investment, and
nearly all organizations have experienced staff reductions during
the recessionary times of the past several years. This means that single
individuals have to wear multiple hats and manage more than one
marketing activity at a time, unlike in the past when a specialist
managed each marketing activity. Marketers still work hard to prepare for the product launches and promotions as they always have.
However, the real work begins once a campaign actually goes live, and
this involves actively tracking campaign results and adjusting those
marketing programs real-time based on that feedback.

Second, the environment is constantly changing, so nimble,
forward-thinking brands are proactively adapting accordingly to the
rapidly changing media environment. These revolutionary marketers
generally spend 50 to 60 percent of their budget at launch. They hold
back 20 to 30 percent of the spend and use it to adjust the campaign
based on performance feedback. They then save the remaining 10 to
20 percent for ongoing testing and measurement of progressive marketing tactics. This approach is virtually the only way that brands can
adapt at scale in today's dynamic environment.

Today brands don't just measure performance in terms of awareness and preference but rather in the form of participant actions.
These require individuals to thoroughly think through desired actions
at the beginning of the campaign rather than at the end. Participant
action planning involves not only developing programs designed to
ignite and inspire participation but also enabling end-to-end tracking,

which is necessary to secure the right data at the right time to track performance. Effective planning also means that a number of departments beyond marketing must work together in an effort to meet participant expectations regarding brand experience and marketers' goals to create fully integrated marketing programs.

If you feel tired after reading this, you are not alone. Marketing in today's environment is anything but a walk in the park. The good news is that because marketing today touches so many departments beyond their own, including customer support, information technology, product marketing, and sales, the department is getting much more visibility and recognition than it did over the past 20 years. It simply cannot be viewed in a silo. Two recent studies indicate that, within five years, chief marketing officers (CMOs) may spend more on technology for marketing than for their information technology (IT) counterpoints. Furthermore, the marketing department is garnering more respect, because companies can track their performance back to marketing activities, even if it isn't based on new models. Demonstrated performance is thought to be the reason that CMOs are keeping their jobs longer, according to a recent study by Spencer Stuart. The average CMO tenure reached 42 months in 2010, seven months longer than the 2009 average and the highest tenure average since Stuart began tracking CMO tenure in 2004. This is largely thought to be the result of brands increasing their spend in digital—a tactic that allows marketers to demonstrate that results of marketing activities are far more impactful than the traditional measures of tracking media effectiveness or share of voice. For the first time, marketers can actually demonstrate their departmental activities' true ROI—and studies indicate that marketing effectiveness or ROI has become the most important consideration in planning marketing investments.

There are plenty of debates about whether marketing should be more art or science. Today's marketing requires an elegant blend of both. The best campaigns are inspiring, creative, and innovative, and they consider actions as part of the overall experience. More marketers are becoming analytically savvy; indeed, some of the most interesting marketers I know began their careers as data scientists. There is no easy, one-size-fits-all approach to measuring marketing, nor is there likely to be one anytime soon.

The Internet Advertising Bureau (IAB), Association of National Advertisers (ANA), and American Association of Advertising Agencies (4A's) have been working on the Making Measurement Make Sense framework, an ecosystem-wide initiative in digital to create a standardized digital measurement framework across platforms. According to the IAB, the Making Measurement Make Sense framework has three primary objectives:

1. Define transparent, standardized, and consistent metrics and measurement systems to simplify the planning, buying, and selling of digital media in a cross-platform world.

2. Drive industry consensus around the solutions.

3. Establish a measurement governance model to support ongoing standards development, ensure compliance, and manage change in a rapidly evolving media climate.

The initiative has yet to gain much traction, despite the fact that the organization made an effort to identify priorities, develop measurement solutions, and build industry consensus in developing Making Measurement Make Sense by assembling a group of 40 thought leaders and decision makers to actively contribute to the initiative. As part of this initiative, these leaders have announced the release of the Guiding Principles of Digital Measurement. These five principles are the foundation of the Making Measurement Make Sense framework and illustrate the complexity of measurement in the current fragmented and dynamic media landscape:

1. Move to a "viewable impressions" standard and count real exposures online.

2. Migrate online advertising to a currency based on audience impressions, not gross ad impressions.

3. Because all ad units are not created equal, create a transparent classification system.

4. Determine interactivity "metrics that matter" for brand marketers so that marketers can better evaluate the online contribution to brand building.

5. Ensure digital media measurement becomes increasingly comparable and integrated with other media.

The IAB is acknowledging that the marketing world is no longer defined solely by impressions; however, the Participation Age is a world of interactions, and not all are paid media. Paid and earned media overlap and have an effect on each other. So, although the IAB guidelines are certainly a step forward in the process, they fall short of solving all marketer problems regarding measurement in our new complex marketing world. The new guidelines account for only the paid portion of the marketing effort. If performance is measured by all participant actions, it's clear why it's so critical to understand how to motivate people to take action—and not just in the form of leads or sales generated by paid media.

The work for marketing performance has just begun. Brands are beginning to understand that all they have known to be true is shifting. They are tackling big challenges, such as the definitions and overlaps of paid, owned, and earned. Even the definition of paid media is changing; Gen Yers are defining it differently, and owned and earned media do not have definitive boundaries. An entire book could be dedicated to performance alone, and it is likely to be rewritten multiple times over the next few years as the media landscape splinters and becomes more dynamic. We will not solve everything here. In the next chapter, much more will be discussed about measurement tools and approaches to help get you started with developing a path toward the future.

Performance Marketing Summary

1. Today's marketer has an even more challenging role—for a number of reasons. First, there are fewer resources dedicated to marketing and digital, despite the increase in digital investment.

2. Second, the environmental is constantly changing. Smart, nimble brands are proactively adapting to the rapidly changing media environment and generally spend 50 to 60 percent of their budget at launch. They hold back 20 to 30 percent of the spend and use it to adjust the campaign based on performance feedback. They then save the remaining 10 to 20 percent for ongoing testing and measurement of progressive marketing tactics. This approach is virtually the only way that brands can adapt at scale in today's dynamic environment.

3. Marketers should not measure performance in terms of awareness and preference only but rather in the form of participant actions. These require individuals to thoroughly think through desired actions at the beginning of the campaign rather than at the end. Participant action planning involves not only developing programs designed to ignite and inspire participation but also enabling end-to-end tracking, which is necessary to secure the right data at the right time to track performance.

4. Effective planning also means that a number of departments beyond marketing must work together in an effort to meet participant expectations regarding brand experience and marketers' goals to create fully integrated marketing programs.

5. The five Guiding Principles of Digital Measurement developed by the IAB, ANA, and 4As illustrate the complexity of measurement in the current fragmented and dynamic media landscape:

   a. Move to a "viewable impressions" standard and count real exposures online.

   b. Migrate online advertising to a currency based on audience impressions, not gross ad impressions.

   c. Because all ad units are not created equal, create a transparent classification system.

   d. Determine interactivity "metrics that matter" for brand marketers so that marketers can better evaluate the online contribution to brand building.

   e. Ensure digital media measurement becomes increasingly comparable and integrated with other media.

11 Planning

Bringing the Participation Way to Life

The first step in embracing the Participation Way begins in a familiar place for marketers who have to create any program with an eye toward strategy and planning. Developing revolutionary marketing programs begins with a solid foundation comprised of insight, documented in a strategy, and brought to life in execution. Even in the Participation Age, there is no substitute for having a brilliant strategy as your foundation. This has been the case for decades, and it will continue well into the future.

Yet unlike many of the language, tools, and marketing approaches developed for advertising and marketing over the years, strategic planning is a relatively recent addition to the marketing toolkit. British advertising agencies in the mid-1960s were the first to develop the early versions of account planning practices. In 1965, Stanley Pollitt, who cofounded Boase Massimi Pollitt (known as BMP) agency, recognized how necessary it was becoming to improve information flow among agencies and clients. The birth of broadcast had heightened the need for more expedient communications among organizations throughout the campaign process. At the same time, research and information were found to be valuable in developing effective creative ideas. So Pollitt suggested that a specially trained research firm work with the account manager as an equal partner—and planning was born.

In 1991, Lisa Fortini-Campbell, a consultant, author, and widely known industry expert, was instrumental in taking planning to the next level. She used her consulting practice, where she worked with a number of multinational companies, including Ford, Kraft, Hewlett-Packard (HP), and Motorola, to advance her theory and recommendations concerning account planning. These recommendations greatly influenced my own perspective about the discipline of strategic rigor for marketing programs; in fact, Fortini-Campbell's values still reside in the process that accompanies the Participation Way. The Fortini-Campbell planning approach consists of five main roles that an account planning process must fulfill:

1. Discover and define the marketing task, organizing information about the customer and the marketplace from every possible source, including data and secondary research.

2. Prepare the strategic brief. This is the tool that the creative and media departments use to bring the program to life. Another main purpose it has is to define the brand's proper positioning.

3. Participate in the creative and media development. It is the account planner's duty to represent the customer during creative and media conceptualization. They may also interact with the creative and media departments through the sharing of initial consumer responses to ad ideas or advertising approaches.

4. Present the ideas to the client. The planner informs the client of "how and why a customer will react to [specific] advertising."

5. Track the program's performance. Through their follow-up research, account planners track reactions to the ads in the actual marketplace and provide all team members with additional information.

The planning function today has evolved to something that is more than the sole responsibility of a planning department, because data and research are so prevalent. Brand organizations are also considering greater integration between functions as well. Historically, there were media experts and there were creative experts, usually held by different individuals with different expertise working with different agencies. Today's breakthrough marketers recognize that it is their responsibility to combine their understanding of participants and the awareness of how they'll use this knowledge within their own businesses, thereby creating a strategic direction and oversight for every marketing program. It is every marketer's job to understand and draw insightful conclusions not only from the participant but also from the competitors and the brand. Often this requires building bridges between departments because organizations are gradually evolving toward better integration, but this is going to take time.

Marketers must distill the great amount of data and information to discover true insight, making the planning function arguably the most important first step. Planning has also become much more dynamic because planners benefit from continual feedback from the current campaign from the time it launches, as well as feedback from previous campaigns and from benchmarking data provided by third parties that provide information about similar campaigns. Despite the vast changes in the quantity and frequency of the input and the fact that the tools of marketing strategic planning have certainly evolved, many marketers are still using a creative brief as the cornerstone starting point for all marketing programs.

The new participation brief has taken cues from the creative brief and been updated to encompass the elements of the Participation Way, focusing less on persuasive communication and more on generating participation. The creative element is still important; as illustrated by Google's Project Re: Brief program, effective marketing programs require a clever story line that stands out in the fragmented and cluttered media environment. The advertising industry as a whole is debating this issue in nearly every industry forum. At the 2012 Cannes Lions festival, there were numerous topics about whether the focus on data is slowly killing creativity as data becomes ever important with the rise of digital marketing and whether creativity is good for effectiveness. Creative is unquestionably an element in effective marketing programs, but perhaps not *the* element.

As touched on previously, developing marketing programs in the Participation Age metaphorically resembles two interconnected wheels (see Figure 6.1). The participant is constantly spinning the wheel on the right, seeking information, asking questions, providing feedback, and so on. The challenge for the brand, represented by the wheel on the left, is to meet the participant's needs by providing information, answering questions, receiving feedback, and connecting to other participants. The goal is to invent marketing programs designed to have an exchange with participants throughout the entire customer life cycle.

The participation planning process was developed in an effort to help brands develop marketing programs designed for the Participation Age by using a set of principles and the Participation Way method. The steps are not that different from traditional marketing planning processes. They allow marketers to develop programs in a way that is easily repeatable and scalable—instrumental elements for teams confronted by economy woes, overloaded teams, and limited budgets. Unlike traditional linear planning processes, participant planning is about a continual improvement approach consisting of three phases: participant and program insight, participation activation, and program improvement or elevation.

The phases are continual; all campaigns begin with the important stage of data and intelligence collection distilled to into actionable insight (see Figure 11.1). The next phase is activation, when participation is activated. The final and third phase, elevate, launches as marketers begin receiving participant feedback on the program and initiate program refinements based on that feedback.

This learning is then channeled back into insights, which, in turn, inform current and future program activation and so on. There are deliverables within each phase that have been highly leveraged from traditional marketing processes but updated and modernized for marketing in the Participation Age. Let's walk through each stage of the process.

Figure 11.1 Participant Planning Process

Insight

The insight phase begins when marketers use the digital tools at their fingertips to collect rich, actionable data that they use to make decisions about the program before the it launches; they continue to collect these data throughout the program's life. As marketers and brands are increasingly participating in social media communities, offline tools and norms no longer apply. Effective engagement requires an authentic and transparent approach based on understanding and respect for the participants, and it provides community for participants as well. We have already discussed the importance and value of listening. Listening can help brands create participant strategies that enable them to proactively inform, educate, influence, and engage. Listening is the first aspect to insight. A brand that learns how to "listen" will add value as it influences more than just marketing.

The listening process begins with aggregating the data for the purposes of developing insight. Technology and platforms now track participant communications and behaviors, which enable brands to incorporate the data to improve media effectiveness. We can view listening as the more qualitative approach to assembling insight. However, it is only one component; data constitute the other. Participants today not only are using technology data to make decisions or access information but are creating it—at an unfathomable pace. These data, at an aggregate level, provide brands with a valuable opportunity to gain insight into what motivates participation.

Former Google chief executive officer (CEO) Eric Schmidt was quoted as saying, "Every two days we create as much information as we did from the dawn of civilization up to 2003." Global market intelligence firm IDC now forecasts that the digital universe will grow 44-fold by 2020, resulting in a total of 35 zettabytes of data in the digital universe. (A zettabyte is equal to 1 billion terabytes; a terabyte is equal to 1,000 gigabytes; and one gigabyte equals 1,000 megabytes.) Although we are all familiar with megabytes—since we have been purchasing computers and storage devices with measurable megabytes for decades—zettabytes are difficult to even comprehend. This amount of data is far more than we ever imagined using for any purpose; I certainly never considered how important data would become to marketing in my lifetime. If this statistic scales at the same rate as the IDC predicts, we could assume that all information from the dawn of civilization up until 2003 will be created every 65 minutes by the year 2020. The challenge and the opportunity for every marketer will then be how to aggregate and translate these data into meaningful insight. The data explosion to the point of being labeled "big data" is the reason many brands are continually struggling with data challenges today. Data can be used for both insight and performance, and, of course, these are connected within the planning life cycle. For simplification purposes, we will focus on data for insight within this chapter and data for performance in the next chapter, which focuses on measurement.

The first step in the insight process is gathering data (both qualitative and quantitative) to be used. Numerous data aggregation and intelligence gathering tools are available in the marketplace today. Several years ago, most companies went through the process of securing a social monitoring partner for their organization. The objective in hiring a partner was to track market perception, largely sentiment. Social monitoring partners generally provide extensive reports. This kind of reporting often provides valuable information, rich with insight potential, in a timely manner. A number of clients have found these reports to be helpful but lacking in delivering actionable insight. This is why the final output of the insight phase is a participation brief. Consistent with developing creative briefs, the planner's role was to work on distilling information into an actionable marketing plan.

Insight by definition is much more than data and information; it is actionable understanding. Gathering and aggregating social and search data are good first steps, but the next step still requires human intervention. It involves cleaning and analyzing this information for relevance and applying marketing knowledge to the process.

Gathering social listening and search information is only the first step. Incorporating marketing effectiveness from current and former campaigns, market knowledge, and competitive intelligence is still important to activating innovative and participative marketing programs, but there are two distinctions in today's insight gathering:

1. **The tools enable information to be gathered in a considerably more scalable, timely manner.** For example, we used to spend weeks, or even months, conducting focus groups to determine emotional attributes associated with a product or service. Today, we can aggregate much of this information using social listening tools and then analyze information to create an effective strategy. The data richness and scale can provide even more effective

results, but data intelligence is raw and lacks the human application to achieve the richness of true insight.

2. **Sophisticated analytics applications now provide insight that is fundamentally invaluable to providing true innovation and performance.** An example of this is how forecasting data from search data may reveal secondary seasonal buying patterns, when tracked over time, that a retailer might not be aware of. Understanding these secondary or tertiary demand opportunities allows marketers to create programs and plan marketing investment timing that might otherwise be missed. Large, seasonal buying patterns such as the winter holiday season or back-to-school time are obvious. However, there is some less obvious seasonality that's actually more common than expected—and that can be an important competitive differentiator for many companies that have a desire to take marketing to the next level or plan investments much more strategically. Sometimes these opportunities are tied to other media activities, such as catalog drops or offline media activities. They can also be tied to events or even a combination of the two. The most famous example of this was highlighted in Bill Tancer's 2008 book *Click*, in which he examined how teen prom magazines drove dress searches earlier in the season than one would intuitively project because the books came out in January, even though most proms are held in May. There are also numerous examples of pop culture events, movies, books, and so on, that drive product sales without brands predicting them. This type of knowledge and activity is influencing many different types of brands. Even pharmaceutical companies are using Google Flu Trends to determine which markets to remind about vaccinations. By monitoring flu searches, the tracking tool can predict where outbreaks are imminent and where they have already occurred. If the outbreak has already happened, public awareness is generally already high because of media coverage

and word of mouth, meaning there is no need to spend money on advertising reminding people to get their yearly vaccine. Conversely, tactically choosing to invest in other markets where outbreaks have not yet happened or are imminent is a better marketing investment and good for the public health as well. These are just a few examples of how using the insight phase can benefit the marketing planning process.

Social media and search can be extremely useful insight tools. Although many marketers use social monitoring to gauge only sentiment, it's widely acknowledged that these tools have low reliability concerning sentiment. In addition, sentiment in and of itself does not provide good guidance on program strategy. Revolutionary marketers, on the other hand, use these tools and search intelligence to gather insight about connecting with participants on a more meaningful level. Tools can aggregate content that marketers can then analyze to determine what people are saying, where they are having conversations (and not just on which social media sites, boards, and so on, but on owned sites, competitor sites, and other such sites), and whether any events drive specific conversations around a product, service, brand, or category.

I cannot emphasize enough the importance of this information in informing a marketing program from the onset. Insight is critical in all types of marketing today, but especially in social environments where engagement is about relationships. Insight involves using data aggregation to build active participant intelligence, which marketers can then use to build participant insight. This exercise used to be referred to as developing personas or consumer portraits; however, we now prefer to create dynamic participant profiles. Portraits and personas seem like static façades or snapshots frozen in time. This worked well for captive audiences who were sitting on the edge of their seats awaiting the next message. But today's environment demands dynamic participant profiles, because these closely resemble constantly moving portraits. They also enable marketers to connect with participants at every critical moment, empower them to engage with their brands, and encourage the brand loyalists to convert others. Similar to the outcome of focus groups of the past, marketers can also use social and search data to determine the emotional triggers that surround a product or service by aggregating and analyzing what people are saying about that product, service, or even brand. The end products of the insight phase are the first iteration of dynamic participant profiles and a participation brief, which incorporates the Participation Way formula and sets the stage to construct program activation.

Activate

The step following a brief creation in traditional advertising is to develop creative concepts. But participation is more than just a creative concept. Participant marketing programs are now an elegant blend of technology, creative, and media, and program activation requires that marketers bring the program to life within the formula framework.

The key to activating participation is empowering participants to pull through the program to next step using the Participation Way formula. The old saying "The media is the message" doesn't work well in the Participation Age. The participants are now the media and the message.

In the activation step, the Participation Way formula—$D + E + C = P2$—comes to life. As we've discussed, the discover principle is about building a program that helps satisfy participants' insatiable need to constantly know about the latest and greatest everything. The participation brief should outline ideas on key triggers to bring discovery to life, helping participants become competent about the product, service, or brand. The empower element is about building programs that inspire action and compel participants to try, share, engage, and provide feedback. Connect requires that we give participants a voice and enable them to build relationships with others around the common interest of that product, service, or brand. Through the creation of environments that foster all three of these elements, the program is more likely to have participation, which, in turn, drives performance.

This might not seem new or different, but rather simply a reframing of how we think about the process. Experience has proved that building these components into the framework provides a more active conversation about the critical elements of the campaign, but it does not require a dramatic change to everything we already know. The purpose of incorporating the Participation Way into the planning process is to ensure that marketers deliberately consider these elements when planning each and every marketing program, rather than just hoping for a "viral hit" without any basis.

Activation allows the Participation Way to affect creative and media. It can be applied at a high level with regard to how to construct overall program elements. It can also be used at the most tactical level, such as search. What keywords and copy have we developed that help people discover more about our product or service? How are we using social assets in the search engine results page to empower participants to share content? Social integration can also be used to inspire participants to connect. Are we developing content for organic search and keywords for paid search that instruct participants where to go to connect others with similar interests?

A visual flow of how the participation and customer life cycle happens is often beneficial to have alongside the participation brief. For many years, marketers have used the purchase funnel as a media tool. And in the past, it's been a valuable way to illustrate how integrated marketing drives messages from one stage to the next. Many have argued that the purchase funnel is dead today—and this is true . . . to a certain extent. There are plenty of indicators pointing to this fact, including a number of variables such as the meandering purchase journey enabled by the mountains of available information and access to retrieval devices and social interactions influencing individual decisions. The funnel becomes problematic when we start using it as a pure metaphor, for example, if a marketer expects zero "spillage" with a literal and linear approach to today's process. It also is problematic when we apply one model to everyone. A number of organizations specialize in data analysis and are seeing early indications that social networks are significantly influencing buying decisions and behaviors. There is no question that buying models will continue to evolve over the next two years as marketers because more savvy at using data and insight for planning and program refinement.

However, I'd like to propose that we don't throw out everything we already know, at least just yet, and still use the funnel today—but with a minor modification. Some models are worth preserving for the time being, simply because they allow meaningful and familiar dialogue, and marketers still need visual tools that enable scalable planning techniques. The purchase funnel remains a relevant tool that aids marketers in planning activities based on different stages around the product life cycle (see Figure 3.1). The only significant adaptation to the funnel visually is the addition of the postpurchase stage. This allows us to view the funnel in a more holistic, three-dimensional view than has been possible in the past. The marketer's goal is to enable action by making the participant an important ingredient in the media and the message. Visually, the new funnel focuses on continual motion, and it is less linear. In the old funnel, a large amount of material—consumers, in fact—were poured in the top, and a few trickled through the bottom. Did you ever wonder what happened to all of those people who just evaporated inside the funnel? The new funnel metaphor is to now to inspire action inside the funnel, where the participants are literally running around, in perpetual action at all stages, including the postpurchase stage. It is now essential to empower participants to become part of the media process.

If our objective is to keep the spiral spinning, we should create campaign programs, assets, and media activities to help drive a successful marketing program that delivers results. When these programs are tied to insight, they are even more powerful. An example that comes to mind is a program we created while working with a company that was well known for a food product whose satisfying aromatic scent caused mouths to water with desire. This brand understood their aromatic power. In fact, their distribution strategy was to locate their retail outlets in heavily populated, but contained, venues, such as shopping malls or airports, where they could release the good smells for everyone to take in, drawing them like flies. What they had not contemplated, until conducting a participation audit, was how scent was associated with memory. All senses have memory links. Many people associate songs to specific events, for example. In this particular case, we were able to use social listening to understand that because this brand's retail outlets are located in airports, many individuals associated the brand with memories of vacations. This was a significant insight, and the brand was able to use it as a building block for creating its participant marketing programs.

Consider all media forms: paid, owned, and earned. Most marketers have embraced the concept that they are no longer responsible only for paid and owned content. Earned content is a vital contributor to overall program management. Dedicating head count and resources to managing earned media has been challenging for brands who are accustomed to traditionally allocating resources based on the size of budgets assigned to individuals. Revolutionary marketers are now calculating the impact of earned media to equate it to overall media value in an effort to champion resources for earned programs.

All traditional mediums now have paid, owned, and earned elements. Search is a great example of a "traditional" digital medium affected by paid, owned, and earned. The search engine results page has always had paid ads on the right rail and at the top, and owned website content has been a consideration for a number of years. However, the engines suddenly are pulling social content onto the page in the "owned" area. This begins to blur the lines between what is paid, earned, and owned, and a number of organizations are already beginning to talk about this within their organizations. Different departments within the organizations have traditionally managed owned and paid search. Some organizations are questioning the value of separating earned and are building it into their fundamental marketing programs. Although it will be some time before these changes begin to affect marketing organizational structures, it will likely happen, and this might be only the beginning of the changes. In fact, given the amount of rapid change in the marketplace, dynamic organizational structures may be here to stay. This is okay as long as the departments work closely together toward a common goal. Progressive marketers are managing paid, earned, and owned search holistically and continually as the earned area, in particular, continues to change and impact search engine results.

The importance of involving participants as part of all marketing programs after they've made a purchase has already been emphasized in previous chapters; marketing is no longer just about influencing a purchase. After-purchase care and management has traditionally been viewed as a different type of marketing activity altogether—and one that's sometimes managed by a different department entirely, such as customer support or customer advocacy. So, in one way or another, many companies treat the customer who has already made a purchase different than a customer prospect. In an environment where conversations, recommendations, and connections are all vital, acknowledging participants after they've made a purchase as being a crucial part of the ongoing purchase process is just good marketing. These individuals provide a critical contribution to the entire customer life cycle. I think we have always believed this to be true, but now more than ever, it's critical to plan for existing customer involvement in the buying process.

Elevate

The elevate phase begins the minute activation occurs, because in today's world, marketers who plan their programs with defined key performance indicators (KPIs) begin receiving immediate feedback as the program goes live. Marketers must define action as performance and must have measurement programs in place. Most marketers understand the importance of measuring marketing success. The economic downturn has spurred the evolution of marketing measurement faster than would have otherwise happened; consequently, most marketing has some form of measurement as part of the initial plan. I often participate as a judge for industry awards and am always amazed at the lack of program measurement, even now. Likewise, many of the programs that do have a measurement component are measuring clicks. It is astounding that our marketing aspiration for the desired participant action is still "to click." We're 15 years into digital with a highly measurable medium, and yet we're still struggling to develop and employ effective measurement approaches to our work. All we can come up with to measure is clicks? Whenever I inquire about this unfortunate occurrence, the question often is, "How can I measure more than that?" This seemingly dead-end question makes things complicated, because it is being asked out of order.

As emphasized previously, the first question a marketer should ask is, "What do I want the participant to do?" This helps both refine the program itself and define the measurement. If you know what you want someone to do, you can determine how you will measure those actions. And, the answer should not be "by clicks." If you are asking someone to go somewhere, of course that begins with a click, but there must be a higher purpose involved. Of course, social is one channel that is more obviously and naturally linked to the idea of participation. And although measuring it has been challenging for most marketers, even Facebook is acknowledging the importance of actions and providing tools that enable marketers to measure performance. The popular social networking site recently launched a program metric called *actions*, which replaces connections in the Ads Manager. For ads and sponsored stories driving to pages, actions records, page likes, page post likes, comments, @mentions, check-ins, photo tags, page post shares, offer claims, question answers, question follows, video views, photo views, link clicks, and page tab views. The challenge is that, although Facebook actions do acknowledge participant behavior as the measurement goal and approach, it's a tracking measure available only inside Facebook walls. This, of course, provides another set of challenges.

Digital is an action-based medium, and actions can be measured. However, understanding the desired action is an important first step. The next step requires that we understand how to get the data at the right time and incorporate it into a dashboard data management tool. Too many marketers focus on glitzy dashboards to solve all of their marketing problems. Defining actions and getting the data are the significant hurdles. Believe it or not, building a beautiful dashboard comes easy once the latter is solved, and dashboards are great at providing quick access to actionable information.

The key to the insight component in planning is to ensure that real-time feedback continually improves overall campaign effectiveness. The beautiful thing about marketing today is that nothing is set in stone—generally—and if something is not working, learning can be leveraged to make adjustments to the existing campaign and planning for future campaigns. As data become more integrated into marketing, our overall perception and approach about how we use it for understanding and planning will change. More often than not, data are still used today to justify what we already understand or expect. Think about our fascination with infographics and dashboards today. They are suddenly appearing everywhere in all forms of media. Infographics don't really reveal anything we don't already know. Similar to the way data are presented in a dashboard, information is conveyed in a more palatable manner so that individuals can digest information quickly and easily. Perhaps the emergence of dashboards and popularity of infographics are a reaction to the data overload we are all experiencing at an ever-increasing pace. A number of individuals believe infographics and dashboards will disappear as quickly as they emerged as we become more comfortable with opening our minds to using data to enlighten us with new information.

Another interesting development in the continually evolving data and measurement world is the study of networks. Over the past five to seven years, there has been a trend to hire mathematics or data experts into marketing organizations. Data and analytics professionals are still hot commodities in the talent marketplace today; however, there is a new and unexpected cast of players just emerging who undoubtedly will also have an impact on marketing in the next five years. A handful of learning institutions and companies are now hiring individuals with network expertise, people who understand connections and circuitry. Can you imagine adding an electrical engineer to your staff? You might in the near future. These revolutionary organizations understand that data and networks will both be instrumental in building knowledge and expertise around the new social and participative environment in the future, and both will be crucial to understanding participation and performance, which is what we will discuss more in depth in the next chapter.

Participant Marketing Summary

1. Developing revolutionary marketing programs begins with a solid foundation comprised of insight, documented in a strategy, and brought to life in execution. Even in the Participation Age, there is no substitute for having a brilliant strategy as your foundation.

2. The Fortini-Campbell planning approach consists of five main roles that an account planning process must fulfill:

   a. Discover and define the marketing task. You must organize information about the customer and the marketplace from every possible source, including data and secondary research.

   b. Prepare the strategic brief. This is the tool that the creative and media departments use to bring the program to life. Another main purpose it has is to define the brand's proper positioning.

   c. Participate in the creative and media development. It is the account planner's duty to represent the customer during creative and media conceptualization. They may also interact with the creative and media departments by sharing initial consumer responses to advertising ideas or approaches.

   d. Present the ideas to the client. The planner informs the client of "how and why a customer will react to [specific] advertising."

   e. Track the program's performance. Through their follow-up research, account planners track reactions to the ads in the actual marketplace and provide all team members with additional information.

3. The new participation brief has taken cues from the creative brief and been updated to encompass the elements of the Participation Way, focusing less on persuasive communication and more on generating participation.

4. The challenge for the brand is to meet the participant's needs by providing information, answering questions, receiving feedback,

and connecting to other participants. The goal is to invent marketing programs that are designed to have continuous exchange with participants throughout the entire customer life cycle. (See Figure 11.1.)

5. Today's environment demands dynamic participant profiles, because these closely resemble constantly moving portraits. They also enable marketers to connect with participants at every critical moment, empower them to engage with our brands, and encourage the brand loyalists to convert others.

6. Unlike traditional linear planning processes, participant planning requires a constant improvement approach that consists of three phases: participant and program insight, participation activation, and program improvement or elevation.

7. The insight phase begins when marketers use the digital tools at their fingertips to collect rich, actionable data that they use to inform make decisions about the program before it launches; they continue to collect these data throughout the program's life.

8. Activation is where the Participation Way formula—$D + E + C = P2$—comes to life. The discover principle is about building a program that helps satisfy the participant's insatiable need to constantly know about the latest and greatest everything. The participation brief should outline ideas on key triggers to bring discovery to life and help participants become competent about the product, service, or brand. The empower element is about building programs that inspire action and compel participants to try, share, engage, and provide feedback. Connect requires that we give participants a voice and enable them to build relationships with others around the common interest of that product, service, or brand. Through the creation of environments that foster all three of these elements, the program is more likely to have participation, which, in turn, drives performance.

9. The elevate phase begins the minute activation occurs, because in today's world, marketers who plan their programs with defined KPIs begin receiving immediate feedback.

10. Data and analytics professionals are still hot commodities in the talent marketplace today. However, there is a new unexpected cast of players just emerging who undoubtedly will also have an impact on marketing in the next five years. A handful of learning institutions and companies are now hiring individuals with network expertise, people who understand connections and circuitry.

12 Measuring Participation Performance

It is becoming more critical to measure marketing performance in this environment of shrinking marketing teams and budgets, a fragmented media landscape, competitive pressures, and an economic downturn. We've already discussed the staggering amount of data available today. The most recent numbers indicate that more than 15 petabytes of new data are generated from both machines and people. (A petabyte is a unit of information equal to 1 quadrillion [short-scale] bytes, or 1,000 terabytes.) And the more we instruments we introduce to the world, the more data will be created.

At the same time, a number of company surveys indicate that senior company executives want their businesses to run on data-driven decisions today but that this is not occurring as often as they'd like given our data accessibility. However, accessibility is not the issue; there are a number of barriers preventing organizations from making decisions and taking actions based on data and insight. And generally speaking, organizational and behavioral barriers, not data obstacles, are holding back widespread adoption.

The first barrier has to do with measurement results appearing in a format that is familiar to the organization. The data and decisions must be linked to business strategy; this is what business leaders know and what they focus on every day. It is also how they are measured on both an individual and organizational basis. The bottom line is that marketing effectiveness ultimately needs to tie back to overall business objectives, and most companies today do not consider customer engagement to be a primary business or marketing objective. Ironically, marketing organizations have done a good job merchandising the fact that either their results can be directly tied to sales or cannot be explained at all, rather than developing a reasonable quantification of return on investment. In either case, this is causing pain within organizations that have few new alternatives; consequently, most remain focused on and organized around products and product sales, not customers.

The second barrier is that, in many cases, the reports and tools implemented to measure marketing are difficult to understand. I can remember when we first began to track and publish marketing results at Hewlett-Packard (HP). I would send the weekly report to HP's Imaging and Printing Group executive vice president once a week. The report was an astounding amount of data: 60 pages or so of intricate campaign measurement details. This was in 2007, when we were just beginning to experiment with how to measure digital media tactics. Executives instinctually understood that data could be insightful to business decision making, and there was a hunger for even the most senior executives to learn from our results.

I was wary of both the dangers and opportunities of this executive-level desire for data and knew from the moment that I hit Send on the e-mail to forward the weekly results that I could expect a call from the vice president asking me to explain a myriad of data nuances in the many charts throughout the report. He was keenly interested in how nearly every page of this information could be used to drive business results. I learned very quickly that I needed to understand not only the depth of the information down to very specific details but also the subsequent action that should be taken (or not taken) as a result of us knowing this information. In order to do that, I was required to thoroughly understand the business and our marketing strategies, which were much larger than just marketing—because this was the language vice president understood. I consequently made a number of adjustments to the format of the report based on how well people could understand or translate it to the organization's accepted language.

Finally, the third barrier, which is highly associated with the first two, has to do with integrating our marketing measurement into familiar organizational processes and approaches. It's difficult to change old habits. A number of research firms have issued studies over the past four to five years that repeatedly indicate that more than 60 percent of marketers still allocate their marketing dollars based on historical spending and are still using historical frameworks to measure their marketing activities. These are the same reasons that, although most marketers no longer see the purchase funnel as accurate, they often still use it today. They do so because it can be measured in a way that most organizations understand, even if it no longer accurately reflects the real buying process. The reality is that there are not many useful or well-understood alternatives.

As we have already discussed, awareness is still important; individuals still need to understand that a product or service exists in order for someone to purchase it, and the end point is still a transaction, because this ties us back to business results. Marketers continue to use mainstream media to inspire consideration. But the passive consumption of media is dying as individuals participate with an ever-increasing number of participant-driven and participant-created resources, such as social networks, online videos, blogs, and review sites. The key distinction lies in the center of the funnel, where participation reigns.

This is where searches, product reviews, recommendations from family and friends, competitive information, and connections with other influencers come into play. It is therefore important to remember that brands are now accountable for not just prospective buyers but also for those who may influence the purchase decision.

A Participation Activation Model (Figure 12.1) has been created by Performics to better illustrate how all of these components work together in the Participation Age. This model can be used to visualize how all components work in our new complex and fragmented marketing landscape.

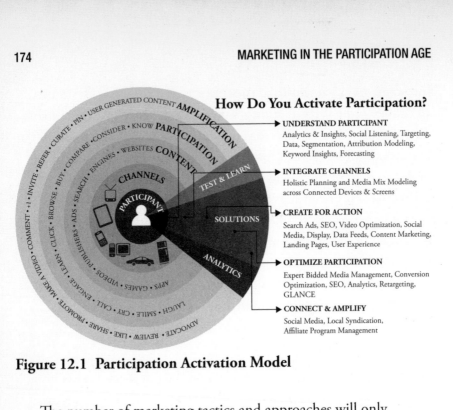

Figure 12.1 Participation Activation Model

The number of marketing tactics and approaches will only increase and become more complex in the Participation Age. As a result, the ever-dynamic digital landscape can potentially lead to misguided and ineffective marketing investments. This is what makes performance an obligation, not just an option, for all marketers. I see too many develop a campaign, and then ask, How will we measure this? If marketers create programs with action in mind using the Participation Way framework and participation brief, they'll already understand what actions they want the participant to take. At this point, it is much easier to determine how to measure those actions.

One of the insights that I had way back in 2007, when we were creating complex measurement and processes, was that measuring performance and gathering and analyzing data have really very little to do with the data, dashboards, and technology or tools. Creating a marketing performance measurement system and approach is truly about people and processes. All the fancy dashboards and technologies in the world cannot compensate for lack of data input from the right person at the right time in the organization. As previously discussed, dashboards tend to tell us what we already understand. Regardless, they are better than not measuring a program at all, so this is where will begin the performance discussion—with how to create a measurement construct for your organization. As such, you need to start with three simple questions:

1. What do we want people to do, or what action do we want them to take?
2. How do we measure those actions?
3. Who has the data to support measurement?

To do this, a campaign owner must coordinate between various parties with different roles and responsibilities within the organization. Far too many marketers struggle with all three components. Many are still creating a communications message instead of taking a participative approach, so they've never considered actions in the program development. This is really the primary first step and the genesis of the Participation Way.

If participation is about actions and measuring actions equals performance, consider the following table, which helps outline how each element of the Participation Way (see Table 12.1) ties to actions and how those actions can be measured.

Once marketers have established the foundations to support actions, the organization's next challenge relates back to measuring performance against business objectives. There are four marketer pain points associated with performance measurement, and they're all about organizational alignment and planning for performance:

1. **The action has been defined, but there is no way to capture the data that allows the marketer to understand what actions the participant is taking or has taken.** This often occurs because

Table 12.1 How to Measure Elements of the Participation Way

	Discover	Empower	Connect
What to track:	Site visits, time spent, pages viewed, search keywords, navigation paths, site log-ins, repeat visitors, unaided awareness	Comments, reviews, likes, shares, forwards, blogs, recommends, opinions, forum discussions, purchases	Online community involvement, sentiment tracking, opinions, customer service calls, net promoter score, product/ service satisfaction
How to track:	Web analytics, media performance	Social media tracking, e-commerce platforms	Brand monitoring, customer service calls, surveys

the vital tagging process has not been planned as part of the campaign approach, and this step cannot happen just as the program is ready to launch. It requires advanced preparation and involves conducting an assessment through stakeholder identification and interviews, as well as assessing the existing reporting view. It also involves assessing and prioritizing actions, since not all actions are created equally. You must give each of them a score in order to prioritize and align the marketing programs and measure accordingly.

2. **Data exist, but you cannot translate data without insight into performance.** There are so many data sources and data reporting companies today. Countless companies have purchased reporting tools or dashboards only to have the reports go unread. Or even worse, the reporting lacks the business context, and insight does not reach the part of the organization that might find value in the outcome. Performance is not about a glitzy dashboard or technology as a sole solution. Because campaigns are still message based, there are rarely advance conversations about what success looks like, or what the goals are for each success metric.

People rarely ask, When are we going to share results and key insights and with whom?

3. **Insight actually exists, but there is no context for it**. As mentioned previously, companies are still organized around products, which means most programs are also in silos. Data and information are plentiful in the Participation Age, and insight can come from a number of areas. However, information cannot be applied unless it is shared. Comprehensive quarterly search results are a mandatory best practice and not just for reviewing past results. This kind of data often reveals insight much richer than just showing how individual search programs are performing. When I worked for HP, I often used search results as a leading indicator for other areas in marketing. For example, what did it say about the marketplace if keyword searches were significantly down quarter after quarter for a particular product category? Had participant behavior and perception shifted? Was a competitor making a move? What could the category managers for that product grouping tell us about other trends they were seeing in the marketplace that, married with the search data, told us a larger story about what was going on? Could this be an early indicator that provided us with information? And had we understood the significance of the insight, could we have made changes that ultimately affected business performance? Despite the effort to connect the dots by providing these data points to other parts of the organization, they were often ignored or individuals were not empowered to act on combining the data. This behavior is slowly progressing today, but rarely at a pace or efficiency that delivers the full opportunity potential.

4. **Organizational discipline to take action is lacking.** Many companies have identified the action, captured the data, and combined it with other data to indicate a trend that provided valuable insight; however, they lack the organizational discipline to take

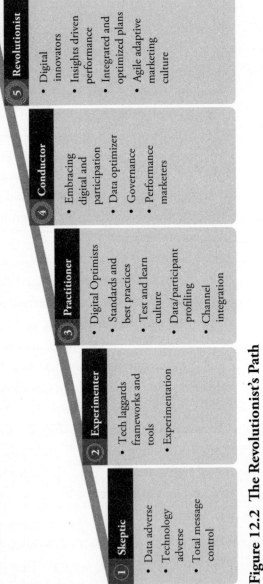

Figure 12.2 The Revolutionist's Path

Note: Performics' Marketer Mind-set is a concept created by Performics to characterize individual marketer's attitudes towards digital marketing at different levels of experience. This concept incorporates language and ideas from Forrester Research, Inc., The Interactive Marketing Maturity Model: November 2008. But the Performics Marketer Mind-set is concept, rather than a quantitative model.

action now that they have it. This is challenging and occurs only in those organizations that are truly revolutionary in their approach to marketing.

At Performics, we call marketers who have become nimble, are data savvy, and understand that taking action will help them to win in the marketplace revolutionists. The Revolutionist's Path (Figure 12.2) was adapted from a 2009 Forrester study depicting how companies are evolving by using data-informed decisions. (The core material and model is copyrighted by Forrester Research, Inc., as The Interactive Marketing Maturity Model, November 2008.) More recently, MIT, Sloan, and IBM conducted a study in 2010 called "The New Path to Value." This study demonstrated that organizations who lead in analytics and data are outperforming their competitors in the marketplace. Marketers find themselves benchmarked at varying stages across different tactics, wherein they may be a "Skeptic" in social media but a "Conductor" in search marketing, according to Forrester Research's Interactive Marketing Maturity Model. Performics believes there is an even-more-advanced marketer who is a revolutionist. For example, revolutionists don't just optimize against data in campaigns; they leverage that data to drive other business decisions such as product development.

The Evolution of the Marketing Revolutionist

The Revolutionist's Path portrays the fast pace at which marketers faced with the economic downturn are reinventing themselves and distinguishing themselves in the marketplace as a result. Marketing revolutionists in the Participation Age are digital innovators who have moved beyond investing the majority of their media spend in digital media and have begun to actually use data insights. They understand that marketing is no longer about persuasion; rather, it is about inviting, engaging, and motivating participation. They have adapted not only their processes but their organizational philosophy in order to be an age-adaptive marketer who is outpacing the competition as a result.

The companies thriving in this new world have embraced a whole new way of doing business, as well as the associated organizational ethos to support this revolutionary approach. I like to say they're nurturists inside because of how they attract and reward employee actions and how they approach their customers and partners. Nurturists are discussed further in the next chapter.

Participant Marketing Summary

1. A number of barriers prevent organizations from making decisions and taking actions based on data and insight. Generally speaking, organizational and behavioral obstacles, not data obstacles, are holding back widespread adoption.

    a. The first barrier for performance measurement has to do with results appearing in a format that is familiar to the organization. The data and decisions must be linked to business strategy; this is what business leaders know and what they focus on every day.

    b. The second is that in many cases, the reports and tools we implemented to measure marketing are difficult to understand.

    c. The third barrier, which is highly associated with the first two, has to do with integrating our marketing measurement into familiar organizational processes and approaches.

2. Start with three simple questions to begin a performance measurement discussion:

    a. What do we want people to do, or what action do we want them to take?

    b. How do we measure those actions?

    c. Who has the data to support measurement?

3. If participation is about actions and measuring actions equals performance, consider the following table, which helps outline how each element of the Participation Way ties to actions and how those actions can be measured (see Table 12.1).

4. There are four marketer pain points associated with performance measurement, and they are all about organizational alignment and planning for performance:

   a. The action has been defined, but there is no way to capture the data that allows the marketer to understand what actions the participant is taking or has taken.

   b. Data exist, but you cannot translate data without insight into performance.

   c. Insight actually exists, but there is no context for it.

   d. Organizational discipline to take action is lacking.

5. Marketing revolutionists in the Participation Age are digital innovators who have moved beyond investing the majority of their media spend in digital media and who actually use data insights. They understand that marketing is no longer about persuasion; rather, it is about inviting, engaging, and motivating participation. They have adapted not only their processes but their organizational philosophy in order to be age-adaptive marketers outpacing their competition.

13 The Future Marketer

The Nurturist

The Participation Age is here for good. Information, communication, and technology have forever changed people and the way in which they relate to products and markets. They have different expectations and different relationships with the companies from which they purchase their products and services. The new participants are more knowledgeable and more demanding than any consumer has been in the past. Using the computers in their pockets, they expect to access what they want, when they want it, 24 hours a day, seven days a week.

The Participation Age has also forever altered the companies that are struggling to thrive in this new world and to deliver their offerings using what they know. Brands are still using the traditional reach broadcast media model whose goal is to reach as many people as possible and try to influence or persuade them about a product or service. Persuasion was always the key skill here, because the message was the most important deliverable. Then, about 20 years ago, we moved into the direct model for marketing to customers. As it was with the reach model, marketers were still in control; this time, however, they used technology and data to choose *which* customers to have a relationship with. Even though it was not really a reciprocal approach, we liked the idea that we could choose the so-called good or right customers for a smart marketing investment—as the media landscape continued to evolve and technology became our friend.

A decade ago, companies began to grapple with the channel changes that the marketplace faced as countless stores transitioned from bricks and mortar to online destinations. We were advising everyone that location no longer mattered. However, we did not consider the unimaginable amount of information that would inform and empower customers—and ultimately placing them in the driver's seat.

Today's environment is more social and communal, more fragmented, more transparent, more personal—and always on. The mobile explosion has also added a layer of complexity, and although location meant nothing 10 years to, it is everything today. For marketers, this has led to the rapid, dynamic, chaotically complex marketplace. There is every indication that the one constant in marketing will be incessant, rapid change.

The forces driving this are much larger than just marketing. Economists have traditionally taught that businesses grow to the point where returns to scale diminish. The reasoning behind this is that the benefits of scale are eventually overwhelmed by the disadvantages of size. Like our weather forecasting models, the stock market, and other methods that were built for an earlier time and place, most economic models were built for a time when communication and transportation were challenges every organization faced, when they were barriers to growth.

But products and services can be accessed and delivered instantaneously and virtually in the Participation Age. Many believe that this is causing impulsive growth that will accelerate, diffuse, and disappear at an equally dizzying pace. Surviving organizations will learn to adapt quickly and continually to these rapid cycle phenomena. Consequently, there is an emergence of an old science called complex adaptive system (CAS) thought to help companies cope with the new dynamic and unpredictable environment. Whether it be the study of CAS or the use of many other new models, overall, there is a movement to embrace more biological, human, and behavioral sciences to solve business problems. Most adaptive system sciences are nonlinear as the growing density of connections, enabled by technology, will continue to create new and more complex models. Many experts believe that as analog and behavior-based ideas take hold in business, the use of machine-based metaphors will quickly fade away and become more biological.

So, what does all this mean for marketing? It means our efforts will need to be grounded in behavioral science and dynamically adaptable—as the Participation Way is. The challenges of managing marketing in this ever-changing media landscape are agonizing and relentless. Rather than viewing marketing as a predictable machine built for the long haul—that is, one that can be turned on and left to run independently—we may need to shift to a more appropriate metaphor—say, for instance, gardening.

Like organizational employee culture, gardens cannot be forced or managed. Although most are planned and cultivated, they are less about predictability and more about nurturing and demand continual care and feeding. The smart gardener is intuitive, is observant, and adapts constantly to what is working by harvesting the yield, culling, and replanting. For the past 60 years, since the birth of television, we have been thriving as hunters by targeting and persuading. In fact, most marketing metaphors were hunter-based. We now need to evolve ourselves to become more like gardeners—nurturing what we've planted. As such, the following five rules apply for nurturist marketing in the Participation Age:

1. **Revolutionary nurturists have embraced test-and-learn values.** They operate in a culture that supports constantly trying new approaches, understanding quickly what works, and immediately scaling, then moving on to the next success. Plant early girl tomatoes alongside the golden cherry variety and watch them closely to see what thrives the best and yields the most. Cull the slow starters and replant. The key is to constantly experiment. Gone are the days of 18 months of marketing planning. In biology, CAS theory teaches us to view systems as groups of individual agents, each acting according to a few basic rules. It is the interaction—the sum of their individual behaviors—that makes the system behave as it does. This is very similar to what happens

in the interconnected world in which we live today. In the Participation Age, both your business and the participant are agents connected in a massive complex system. A very small deviation can create a large impact, so constantly testing, learning, and scaling is the key to success. Revolutionary marketers reserve a minimum of 10 percent of their marketing budgets for testing and learning. When they find something that works in a test, they immediately scale. When the results start to fade, they move on, and this is easy because they always have a stack of new opportunities in the queue. A number have benefited from this approach and are now looking to increase that to nearly 30 percent. This has also affected the planning and processes on the agency side. It means continually investing both in early innovation and in talent knowledge and training because of the dynamic environment externally and internally. As our economic cycles occur at a more rapid rate and affect the increasingly complex media landscape, this will become a common practice for marketers—and the percentage of marketing dedicated to continual testing may even approach 50 percent or more.

2. **Innovate; don't perfect.** Cultures intrinsically connected with nature are in tune with the fact that there is beauty in imperfection. For example, citizens of Japan have practiced the ancient ritual of the tea ceremony for more than a thousand years. They pour powdered green tea in bowls called chawan. Some bowls were created nearly half a century ago, amazing artifacts that were hand thrown by potters who often spent a lifetime perfecting their creations. As the bowls were fired in kilns, flaws occurred in the finish. Rather than throwing the imperfect bowls out, they were revered and valued because of their individuality. As the master would extend the bowl of tea to a guest, he would rotate the bowl so that a tiny flaw or imperfection in the finish would be *visible* to the guest. The flaws weren't something to hide;

rather, they represented the unpredictable forces of nature. In much the same way, Participation Age nurturists realize that it's better to leverage from the best at the moment, quickly adding value before someone else does it first. The concept of continual innovation is crucial, because the best may not last long. Developing a marketing program that never ends is the new way of marketing. Think again of the spiral and the Participation Activation Model. The Participation Way framework is about human behavior and is by design more biological than scientific or mechanistic. Don't spend months looking for the perfect big idea, because this notion is highly flawed. Your competitors may have four innovative ideas before you find the perfect big one. Pick something that's good enough and embrace the flaw as an opportunity to learn. Adapt quickly and move on.

3. **Act quickly and motivate others, including participants, to act on your behalf.** The Participation Way framework is built on exactly this principle. Understanding how to motivate people to do something is crucial to today's successful marketing programs. The same is true for marketers who wants to inspire their organizations. Just *do something!* Encourage those in your organization to act quickly and create an environment that rewards moving quickly. If the aphids are eating your plants, bring in ladybugs—today, not tomorrow. Water every day with the approximate amount using judgment. Don't spend time measuring each portion of water a teacup at a time to perfect the amount. Estimate and act; because if you don't, your competitors will.

4. **Mix and blend; don't invent.** Nature is about constantly mixing things up and trying things out to make new ones. Partner with others to create unique solutions that might benefit your brand, product, or solution. Again, this rapid cycle environment will create numerous opportunities to ride a wave; when results begin to diminish, it's time to move on. Leverage the test-and-learn

approach to ensure you have a suite of opportunities in the wings that are ready to ride the next big wave. When I left Hewlett-Packard (HP) and entered the agency world working at Moxie Interactive, I ran the department within the agency responsible for trends, research, and analytics. The trends team was focused on constantly monitoring the digital and media landscape and setting up meetings with potential partners to determine who might be viable new partners for our clients. These trendspotters, as we called them, also were assigned specific brands so that they could evaluate partners with individual brand needs in mind. This work was valuable to brands; the landscape is moving so quickly that having someone constantly monitoring the space and bringing opportunities was a key competitive differentiator. Many brands paid for this activity to occur within the agency partner because they did not have the bandwidth or expertise within their own group. It also was valuable for the agency because most agencies are famous for not investing in new products, services, or partnerships until after a client has agreed to pay for it. This usually means that the agency and marketer are scrambling at the last moment. Therefore, having a team that focused on trends and the future kept the agency current and prepared. Choose an agency partner who is pushing the envelope and remember to consider technology, media, and creative opportunities. Remember, the most elegant marketing programs are elegant blends of all three.

5. **Embrace failures as gifts in the pursuit of results.** In order to champion the previous four rules, your company will need to adopt an "embrace risk and champion failures" culture. Organizations need to learn from their mistakes and accept that failures are inevitable in finding success. Revolutionary marketers understand the importance of risk taking to delivering results. The reason is simple: it often takes several failures to find the opportunities that yield the best results. For example, we recently worked with a major retailer who understood that a twice-yearly

catalog generated a significant sales demand opportunity that paid search could capture within three weeks after the catalog shipment. Capturing demand is the easy; however, doing so while maintaining campaign efficiency is much more difficult. The team failed at four different campaign methodologies before they found a winner by matching the right combination of variables to capture significant demand for the client without compromising results. This particular client is willing to endorse responsible risks because the organization recognizes the potential reward—and also recognizes that failure is part of the journey to success. It's important to ensure there is a true partnership for this approach. Agencies who are willing to put skin in the game and get paid only if they deliver results demonstrate commitment to the partnership. Providing these results for clients—and embracing failure along the way—is also part of the culture of the future. This is an important consideration when partnering for risk returns. Shared risk and shared values are vital in every partnership.

It's clear that we are living in a highly participative and networked environment—and we, as marketers, must accept we are not in control. We have moved beyond the phase where reach, frequency, and the big idea are the "secrets" to persuading someone to take action. Even the media belongs to the participants now, as they manage the networks. The fascination of one-to-one marketing has faded because the marketer no longer can choose which participants to target. The participants, not the marketers, are in control, and they are demanding a *relationship*, not just a marketing message. A relationship is reciprocal and requires a value exchange. If participants don't find value in the relationship, then they move on. The choices and opportunities are theirs.

Marketing in the Participation Age requires new dynamic and nonlinear models. *Now* is the time to evolve. I cannot imagine working in a more challenging and yet exciting time for marketing.

You can help lead a revolution in your organization. It sometimes seems like an unattainable goal, but one person can make a difference—and you are not alone.

Sometimes, a little inspiration goes a long way toward creating a ripple that becomes a tidal wave. In the fall of 2011, I had the privilege of attending Google's annual Zeitgeist event in Scottsdale, Arizona. One of the many brilliant speakers sharing his thoughts and ideas with the Zeitgeist crowd was 83-year-old political scientist Dr. Gene Sharp. Dr. Sharp has been a professor of political science at the University of Massachusetts Dartmouth since 1972. He is considered a revolutionist expert, so his thoughts were particularly timely considering 2011 was a productive year for revolutionists around the world. In fact, his life's work has just been made into a documentary film titled *How to Start a Revolution*.

Dr. Sharp's remarkable career consists of providing the design for the revolutions in Serbia, Ukraine, Guatemala, and Indonesia and, most recently, serving as the inspiration behind the activists who launched the Arab Spring. Sharp has been writing prescriptive books for successful revolutionaries for the past 50 years. His most famous work, *From Dictatorship to Democracy*, written in 1993, outlines 198 methods of nonviolent resistance. It's been described as "more powerful than any bomb" and has been subsequently banned in a number of countries. Despite his controversial writings, Dr. Sharp's message was clear: every person makes a difference, and motivation to action is the key. Every single marketer is also an agent in our own system and our own industry. One person and one act can make a difference and can effect change.

I hope that this book has provided the information, knowledge, and insight for you to feel empowered and inspired to take part. You are not alone. Others are out there looking for other revolutionaries to join the cause. The Participation Age is upon us. Now is the time. You are the difference. You are a participant.

Participant Marketing Summary

1. Today's environment is more social and communal, more fragmented, more transparent, more personal—and always on.

2. The mobile explosion has also added a layer of complexity; although location meant nothing 10 years to, it is *everything* today. This has led to a rapid, dynamic, chaotically complex marketplace. There is every indication that the one constant in marketing will be incessant, rapid change.

3. Rather than viewing marketing as a predictable machine built for the long haul—that is, one that can be turned on and left to run independently—we should shift to a more appropriate metaphor—say, for instance, gardening. Like organizational employee culture, gardens cannot be forced or managed. Although most are planned and cultivated, they are less about predictability and more about nurturing demanding continuous care and feeding. The smart gardener is intuitive, is observant, and adapts constantly to what is working by harvesting the yield, culling, and replanting.

4. We now need to evolve ourselves to become more like gardeners— nurturing what we've planted. As such, the following five rules apply for nurturist marketing in the Participation Age:

   a. Revolutionary "nurturists" have embraced test-and-learn values. They operate in a culture that supports constantly trying new approaches, understanding quickly what works, and immediately scaling, then moving on to the next success.

   b. Innovate; don't perfect. Cultures intrinsically connected with nature are in tune with the fact that there is beauty in imperfection, and marketers can learn from this.

   c. Act quickly and motivate others, including participants, to act on your behalf.

    d. Mix and blend; don't invent. Nature is about constantly mixing things up and trying things out to make new ones. Partner with others to create unique solutions that might benefit your brand, product, or solution.

    e. Embrace failures as gifts in the pursuit of results. In order to champion the previous four rules, your company will need to adopt an "embrace risk and champion failures" culture.

5. Marketing in the Participation Age requires new dynamic and nonlinear models. *Now* is the time to evolve.

6. Every person makes a difference, and motivation to action is the key. Every single marketer is also an agent in our own system and our own industry. One person and one act can make a difference and can affect change.

7. You are not alone. Others are out there looking for other revolutionaries to join the cause. The Participation Age is upon us. Now is the time. You are the difference. You are a participant.

REFERENCES

Belleghem, Steven Van, "InSites Consulting Social Media Around the World Study," http://www.slideshare.net/stevenvanbelleghem/social-networks-around-the-world-2010.

Campbell, Lisa-Fortini. (2002). Hitting the Sweet Spot: How Consumer Insight Can Inspire Better Marketing and Advertising. *Journal of Consumer Marketing*, 9(4), 73–74.

comScore Research, The 2009 U.S. Digital Year in Review: A Recap of the Year in Digital Marketing, February 2010; Power of Like and Power of Like2 (2012), U.S. Power of Like series, a research collaboration between comScore and Facebook to deliver unique insights on the impact of social media marketing. Available at http://www.comscore.com.

CNW Research. "Automotive Industry Tracking," accessed 2010; ongoing studies "Internet: General and Automotive Searches." www.cnwmr.com.

Deci, Edward L., and Ryan, Richard M. *Intrinsic Motivation and Self-Determination in Human Behavior* (New York: Plenum Press, 1985): 113–125.

Deci, Edward L., and Ryan, Richard M. University of Rochester. "Self Determination Theory: An Approach to Human Motivation and Personality," accessed 2012, www.selfdeterminationtheory.org.

Experian, "Digital Marketer Trend and Benchmark Report," accessed 2010, http://go.experian.com/forms/experian-digital-marketer-2012.

Gellner, Ernest, *Words and Things: A Critical Account of Linguistic Philosophy and a Study in Ideology* (London: Gollancz, 1959).

Gutman, J. (1982). A Means-End Chain Model Based on Consumer Categorization Processes. *Journal of Marketing*, 46(2), 60–72.

Hull, C. L., *Principles of Behavior: An Introduction to Behavior Theory* (New York: Appleton-Century-Crofts, 1943).

IBM, "From Stretched to Strengthened: Insights from the Global Chief Marketing Officer, October 2011," accessed 2012. www-935.ibm.com/services/us/cmo/cmostudy2011/cmo-registration.html.

Ipsos, "OTX MediaCT Longitudinal Media eXperience Study," accessed 2011, www.ipsos-na.com/news-polls/pressrelease.aspx?id=4957.

Jenkins, Henry, *Convergence Culture: Where Old and New Media Collide* (New York: New York University Press, 2006).

Jenkins, Henry, "If It Doesn't Spread, It's Dead (Part One): Media Viruses and Memes," *Confessions of an Aca-Fan* (blog), February 11, 2009, http://henryjenkins.org/2009/02/if_it_doesnt_spread_its_dead_p.html.

Kettering, Charles F., "Keep the Consumer Dissatisfied," *Nation's Business* 17, no. 1 (January 1929).

Krugman, Herbert E., "The Impact of Television Advertising: Learning without Involvement," *The Public Opinion Quarterly,* 29, no. 3 (Autumn, 1965): 349–356.

Leach, William R., *Land of Desire: Merchants, Power, and the Rise of a New American Culture* (New York, Vintage Books, 1993).

L2ThinkTank, "Facebook IQ," accessed 2012, www.l2thinktank.com/research/.

McCarthy, E. Jerome, *Basic Marketing: A Managerial Approach* (Homewood, IL: Irwin Publishing, 1975).

North American Technographics, "Interactive Marketing Online Survey, Q2," (survey, 2009).

O'Reilly, Tim, and Battelle, John, "What Is Web 2.0?" last updated September 30, 2005, http://oreilly.com/web2/archive/what-is-web-20.html.

Pew Internet and American Life Project, "The Rise of the 'Connected Viewer,'" accessed 2012, http://pewinternet.org/Reports/2012/Connected-viewers.aspx.

Performics and ROI Research, "S-Net: A Study in Social Media Usage and Behavior," accessed 2012, www.performics.com.

Performics, "Activating Participation Model," 2012, www.performics.com.

Rogers, Simon, *The Facts are Sacred: The Power of Data* (London, UK: Guardian Shorts, 2012).

Rushkoff, Douglas, *Media Virus: Hidden Agendas in Popular Culture* (New York: Ballantine, 1994).

Schmidt, Eric, Speaking at Technonomy Conference, Lake Tahoe, CA, August 4, 2010.

Sharp, Gene, *From Dictatorship to Democracy: A Conceptual Framework for Liberation* (East Boston, MA: Albert Einstein Institute, 2003).

Singletary, Michelle, "It's Time to Drop the Consumer Label," *Washington Post*, January 4, 2009.

Spencer, Stuart, "Annual CMO Study," accessed 2010, www.spencerstuart.com/research/cmo/1329/.

Stearns, Peter, N., *Consumerism in World History: The Global Transformation of Desire* (New York: Routlege Taylor and Francis Group, 2001).

Tancer, Bill, *Click: What Millions of People Are Doing Online and Why It Matters* (New York: Hyperion, 2008).

Woolf, Virginia, *Mr. Bennett and Mrs. Brown Essay* (first published by Criterion, 1928) (New York: Hogarth Essays, 1924).

Yankelovich Research, "The Futures Company, Research Study," accessed 2007, www.thefuturescompany.com.

ZenithOptimedia, "Quarterly Ad Expenditure Forecast, London, UK," accessed June 2012, http://www.zenithoptimedia.com/zenith/zenithoptimedia-releases-new-ad-forecasts-global-advertising-continues-to-grow-despite-eurozone-fears/

INDEX